Follow Your Heart

RECIPES FROM
FOLLOW YOUR
HEART'S KITCHEN

Cookbook

Janice Cook Knight

Illustrations by Kristine McCallister

WILEY

JOHN WILEY & SONS, INC.

Published by John Wiley & Sons, Inc., Hoboken, New Jersey
Published simultaneously in Canada

LIBRARY OF CONGRESS CATALOGING-IN-PUBLICATION DATA:

Cook Knight, Janice.
Follow your heart cookbook : recipes from Follow Your Heart's kitchen / Janice Cook Knight ; illustrations by Kristine McCallister.
    p. cm.
Includes bibliographical references and index.
ISBN 0-7645-7686-0 (pbk. : alk. paper)
1. Vegetarian cookery. 2. Follow Your Heart Natural Foods Restaurants (Firm) I. Follow Your Heart Natural Foods Restaurants (Firm) II. Title.
TX837.C5975 2005
641.5'636—dc22

2005004380

Book design by Richard Oriolo

Printed in the United States of America

10 9 8 7 6 5 4 3 2 1

Follow Your Heart
Cookbook

Contents

Preface

IN THE EARLY YEARS OF FOLLOW Your Heart, there was another vegetarian restaurant in the San Fernando Valley. We weren't really competitors,
because that's not the vegetarian way, but we feigned a sort of mock rivalry,
complete with the obligatory annual softball game. The name of that restaurant
was Our Contribution. I always thought it was a great name for that type of
enterprise, because truly that is what each of us is doing in a service business—
making a contribution.

In a similar sense, that is the intention of this book. In the vast universe of cooking, what more could any one book do than simply make a contribution to the
body of knowledge that already exists? Within our small restaurant alone, so
much has been done over the years, by so many people. Only a fraction of it
could practically be presented in a single volume. Our menu is regularly changed
as tastes evolve; the purpose of this book is neither to set down all the recipes
from Follow Your Heart's menu, nor to document the thousands of recipes for
dishes we have prepared over the years. Instead, the *Follow Your Heart Cookbook*

honors the many requests for a comprehensive cookbook from our restaurant—one that goes beyond our soup recipes in the popular *Follow Your Heart's Vegetarian Soup Cookbook*.

The perfect person to write the book was Janice Cook Knight, a former Follow Your Heart chef, and currently a cooking teacher and writer. For Janice, who also wrote the restaurant's original soup cookbook, this book is, without a doubt, a labor of love and devotion. Painstakingly crafted over years, amidst all the day-to-day demands of a busy life, each recipe was tested time and again, by herself and others, to ensure a final recipe that was true to the original.

While most of the recipes in this book are from Follow Your Heart, many also come from Janice's extensive experience outside of the restaurant. As people who are passionate about food, we often come across recipes that we'd like to use but can't, due to some ingredient that doesn't fall within our standards of what's natural or vegetarian. You'll find some recipes adapted from more traditional cookbooks, such as the Tofu Marbella (page 140), adapted from the *Silver Palate Cookbook* and originally using chicken.

Over the years, I have spoken with thousands of people—often during job interviews at Follow Your Heart—concerning their choice of a vegetarian diet. One thing I believe I have learned is that there are no two vegetarians exactly alike. There are unique and personal reasons why each individual has come to adopt a vegetarian diet and lifestyle, as well as specific parameters they've chosen to follow.

Follow Your Heart is a lacto-vegetarian restaurant. That means we don't serve meat, poultry, fish, or eggs, but we do include dairy products. As vegetarian standards go, that's a fairly middle-of-the-road position. I've encountered people who consider themselves vegetarians because they rarely eat red meat, but include just about everything else. On the other hand, a considerably stricter interpretation is the vegetarian known as a "vegan." *Vegan* is a word that has come into use more recently and is an increasingly popular vegetarian standard. In addition to avoiding all flesh foods, vegans also exclude eggs, dairy products, and sometimes honey. Many of our menu items and cookbook recipes are appropriate for a vegan diet.

While none of the recipes in this book include eggs, many do utilize dairy products or honey. For simplicity, each recipe does not state all of the possible alternatives. For example, every time a recipe calls for butter, it does not also say "or non-hydrogenated margarine." Vegetarians are already quite adept at making the appropriate substitution. We hope readers will recognize that in not always listing the vegan ingredient, we are not making a statement of preference for one over the other as much as we are using the ingredients that we feel would most likely be chosen by the greatest number of readers.

For years we have observed as first-time customers walk into our store or restaurant, a quizzical expression on their faces as if to say, "What *is* this?' Often one foot is slightly inclined toward the exit. Many of us remember being in that same position, not wishing to reveal how strange and unfamiliar it all looked to us. That's why the first word on our restaurant menu is "Welcome.' Perhaps as a result of this approach, a visit to Follow Your Heart has indeed been that first step for many into the world of natural foods or a vegetarian diet. This, in fact, is what we see as our mission, moving forward with the addition of this new book, the *Follow Your Heart Cookbook—our* contribution.

BOB GOLDBERG (Co-founder)
Follow Your Heart

You can find us at:

Follow Your Heart
21825 Sherman Way
Canoga Park, CA 91303
818-348-3240

www.followyourheart.com
or e-mails to: info@followyourheart.com

Acknowledgments

THE SEEDS FOR THIS BOOK were planted many years ago with the help of Kristine McCallister and Kathy Goldberg. Several of their recipes (and Kristine's illustrations) grace these pages. I am very grateful to both of you for your ongoing friendship, laughter, boundless creativity, and encouragement.

Bob Goldberg and Paul Lewin both recognized and understood my passion for food, cooking, and sharing it with others through the medium of the restaurant and later, the cookbooks. Thanks to you both (and also to former partners Michael Besancon and Spencer Windbiel) for giving me a great place to play with the foods I love, as well as a community of kindred spirits and friends. Bob, a heartfelt thank you for the opportunity to write another book for Follow Your Heart. Your faith and patience are admirable, and you have acted as a touchstone and a sounding board, as well as my longtime friend. And thank you for your thoughtful preface, and for contributing Follow Your Heart's interesting history.

Lucie Curtiss, thank you so much for guiding my manuscript into the capable hands of Anne Ficklen at Wiley. It was a serendipitous delivery. Anne, it has truly been a pleasure working with you and your staff; sometimes good things take a while, and I now can truly appreciate all the time and thought that have gone into turning the manuscript into a real book. Thank you also to the art and production department at Wiley, who spent so much time working to produce the design. And thank you to Ward Schumaker for the cover we all love.

A very personal thank you to my husband Jim Knight, who loves helping people do what they love to do—I am a happy recipient; thanks to our children: Tricia, Paul, Mathew, and Sarah, enthusiastic tasters (and fearless critics); thanks to Kim Schiffer who hears and tastes it all, and always returns a kind and illuminating response; thanks to my sisters: Linda Cook for testing some of the recipes and giving valuable feedback, and Pamela Cook for ongoing vegetarian enthusiasm; thanks to John-Roger for keeping the process so simple; thank you Breck Costin for clearing the way to the work. Thank you also to Stacy Wyman, for sharing your recipes and friendship; Jasprit and Teresa Singh, for sharing your delightful mother and her recipes with me; Howard Schiffer, who willingly lends an ear and lots of love; Dale Migliaccio and Laurie Dean, for your ongoing support in many arenas; Pamela Sheldon-Johns, for the teaching opportunities, cookbook advice, and a wonderful Italian experience; Dennis Dalrymple, master of the book contract; Diane Jacobs and Carol Bidnick, for valuable editing advice and referrals. Thank you Deborah Madison for your generous comments and referrals and for taking the time to look the book over closely in the midst of a busy schedule. A hug and a big thank you to Bruce Gelfand: you helped me say it better, and your enthusiasm always inspires.

Thank you to the many Follow Your Heart chefs who contributed recipes. While I can't name you all here, I am grateful for the legacy of recipes that continues to grow and thrive in the Follow Your Heart experience. Thank you David Spain for your long contribution and personal help with the recipes.

And to our loyal customers: Without you, Follow Your Heart wouldn't be here. Thank you for understanding, enjoying, and loving what we do. Your continued response and support keep us cooking and inventing every day.

Some of you even contributed comments for the book cover: Kevin Eubanks, Mike Farrell, Kevin Nealon, Howard Lyman, and others…I'm sorry there wasn't room to use everything you wrote, but your support means so much to us. Thank you.

JANICE COOK KNIGHT

IT'S A HUMBLING PROCESS TO attempt to thank all who deserve acknowledgment for the success of a collaborative project, especially one such as this book, which has involved so many people and spanned so many years. Janice Knight, whose vision commitment, and unwavering determination kept this project alive through its completion, has been an absolute inspiration to me in the art of never, ever, ever giving up. I have known few people in my life who only need to show up to brighten the day. Jan is clearly one of those. Working with you on this project, Jan, has been a totally joyful experience. I want to thank you for always keeping that connection to "The Heart" in your heart.

To Kristine McCallister, whose contributions to Follow Your Heart go far beyond the beautiful illustrations within this book, you can never fully appreciate the impact of the beauty you have left in your wake. Thank you for your drawings, your recipes, your humor, and your love.

To my wife Kathy, also once one of the gifted Follow Your Heart chefs, your contributions, which go so far beyond the wonderful recipes you have given us, continue to nourish the magic that is the essence of "The Heart." Thank you for supporting and sharing my dreams.

My former partners and founders Michael Besancon and Spencer Windbiel have long since moved on, but without them, there would have been no Follow Your Heart. Much of what exists today is the reverberation of a bell which we once rang together. While today, Paul and I are the guardians of that treasure, we will never forgot the bond that we forged as we built it. Ah, those were the days!

Paul Lewin, the fourth founder, and my current partner and best friend for over forty years, you are the kindly and loving lion who would never let us fail. There is not space here to thank you for all you have given, but let it be said that without you, "The Heart" would not be the same. Your strength is that you believe in people, and when people know that someone believes in them, they do accomplish great things.

In that same vein, I want to acknowledge the talented people at John Wiley & Sons, our publishers, especially Anne Ficklen, whose e-mails in pursuit of this project could be their own book, and whose great efforts were only matched by the warmth and good cheer which came carefully packed within each message. Anne, I believe that from four thousand miles away, you came to understand the essence of Follow Your Heart. Thank you for helping us to produce a book which is true to that spirit.

To the cooks, managers, artists, customers, the hundreds of others whose names could fill pages here, but whom I will not even attempt to list because this list could only be incomplete, I acknowledge you for your gifts and contributions. I trust that the memory of the part that you played is itself a lasting reward. For myself, I will treasure it, and you all, forever.

BOB GOLDBERG

Introduction

I LOVE FOOD. YOU COULD SAY I'm obsessed with food. I love to cook everything, but I have a special passion for vegetables.

Vegetarian cookbooks are often my favorites. Vegetarians think differently than omnivores: Limitation creates inspiration. When you take the meat out of the recipe, your mind runs in creative directions.

Take soup stock. I can't tell you how many recipes call for chicken stock as the liquid ingredient—which is fine, except that it makes everything taste like chicken. Soups made from vegetables take on an entirely different character: Mushroom Stock (page 107), for example, adds incredibly rich flavor to soups or risottos. But if you are not a vegetarian, you might never consider it.

I cooked at Follow Your Heart's vegetarian restaurant for many years. This taught me great flexibility in the food world—freedom to substitute tofu or tempeh in recipes calling for chicken, to substitute soymilk or rice milk in recipes calling for regular cow's milk, or to use spelt, barley, or rice flour instead of wheat flour in a pie crust. We live in such a "wheaty" culture, yet there are so many other available grains. Why not make tabbouleh salad with quinoa (page 62) instead of bulghur wheat?

The restaurant at Follow Your Heart has never used eggs, and neither does this cookbook. You can make many wonderful baked goods and other recipes without them, including cakes, pancakes, and even an eggless Spicy Hollandaise Sauce (page 51). As with taking chicken stock out of soup, when you refrain from baking with eggs, other flavors become more pronounced.

If you're feeling hungry, let's visit Follow Your Heart's restaurant.

Sidle up to the long counter, where a blackboard menu offers the best cup of soup this side of the Rockies, and soup is served all day. There are usually two or three to choose from, such as Sweet Corn Velvet Soup (page 104) or Great Northern Beans and Greens Soup (page 100).

For breakfast, you might order Blue Cornmeal Flapjacks (page 38), Tofu Benedict (page 49), or Olallieberry Bran Muffins (page 29). Lunch might be The Reuben Sandwich (page 96, vegetarian of course), Easier Caesar (page 60), or a sandwich of Roasted Eggplant, Leeks, and Italian Cheeses on Cornbread (page 91). The dinner menu offers one special each evening, in addition to our regular items: from Pad Thai (page 131) to pizza, stir-fries to Savory Vegetable Cobbler (page 127).

Follow Your Heart is also a natural food store. Take a walk with me down the aisles of our grocery.

Produce is my favorite place to start. Let the fruits and vegetables call to us. Are you craving fresh chard, sautéed and sprinkled with balsamic vinegar? Farm fresh tomatoes, sliced and garnished with basil and fresh mozzarella? The eggplants are plump and purple, with tight, shiny skins—a sign of freshness (try Rolled Eggplant Stuffed with Goat Cheese and Herbs, page 8). Late summer brings butternut squash and the large Tahitian squash that looks like a caveman's club, and weighs about as much; either would be delicious in our Butternut Squash Soup (page 98). Potatoes in shades of red, yellow, and brown are in ample supply (try them in Roasted Potato and Watercress Salad, page 64). D'Anjou pears would make a great Pear Crostata (page 166) with a bit of fresh ginger.

Moving deeper into the store, we pass the bulk bins with their various treasures: dried beans in jewel tones, whole grains, flours, and cereals. An array of the organic cheeses holds court near many kinds of tofu—firm, soft, plain, and seasoned. Around the corner are freshly squeezed juices, everything from orange to carrot to mixed greens to watermelon. Every conceivable kind of milk and organic butter and soy or rice or multigrain beverage is there as well. Pick up a gorgeous loaf of whole grain bread—there are many different kinds: sprouted, or yeast-free, or made from spelt, rye, rice, or wheat. Purchase nut butters made from cashews and sunflower seeds as well as organic roasted peanut butter. Sweeteners of honey, maple, or cane, to name a few, will help us make our own delicious baked goodies at home. In short, everything you need to make the recipes in this book.

I live in Santa Barbara now, where we are blessed with several farmer's markets each week. I rarely buy fresh tomatoes from the end of November, when they disappear at the farmer's markets, until June or July, when the new crop comes in. It isn't a sacrifice; tomatoes don't usually taste as good at other times of the year. But some other delicious vegetable or fruit will be around during those other months to entice me.

I love to feel the seasons change, to taste the foods that come with them. Vegetarianism connects me with the seasons—the vast glorious world of food.

Come cook with me: We will think like vegetarians.

The Story of Follow Your Heart

"It was late spring, 1970, and flower power was in full bloom. It was a magical time that inspired many of us to believe that we could change the world. In retrospect, I believe we did."

In those days, health foods could be found only in small shops, which were primarily vitamin stores. There wasn't much organic produce. There wasn't much of anything. But if you were inclined to eat something as strange as, say, yogurt or wheat germ, these items couldn't be found in your local supermarket. Only health food stores dabbled in such things.

This was the way the world was in the spring of 1970, when Michael Besançon, a young hippie and spiritual seeker, began a seven-seat juice and sandwich bar, operating it as a concession in the back corner of a 1300-square-foot health food store in Canoga Park, California.

The business was started with a whopping initial investment of $250 and 20 books of Green Stamps, redeemed for essentials. Plates, utensils, and glassware, none of which matched, were garnered from the many thrift stores that dotted the neighborhood, known for its antique shops and vintage apparel. The store was called Johnny Weismuller's American Natural Foods, after the Tarzan movie star and Olympic swimming champion, who had licensed his name to the store's owner. Local patrons affectionately referred to the place simply as "Johnny's."

Although the store sold meat, Michael's spiritual views were reflected in the food concession's lacto-vegetarian menu. The philosophy was to serve generous portions of home-style cooking, and to treat every person who came into the store as your brother or sister. An enormous avocado sandwich was 65 cents, a cup of hearty soup was 20 cents, and if you ordered "The Love Plate," you'd get both, plus a fresh juice, all for $1.00. Needless to say, it wasn't long before there was a line out the door.

In the spring of 1971, Michael accepted the job of store manager, and hired Bob Goldberg, a regular customer, to help with operating the food bar. Over the next couple of years, Bob brought in his friend Paul Lewin, and Michael recruited his friend Spencer Windbiel to work in the rapidly growing enterprise. In November 1973, the four pooled their resources and bought the store. Because they were doing what they believed in, they named their business Follow Your Heart.

Disregarding the conventional wisdom of those in the health food industry, the partners decided to eliminate meat, poultry, and fish from the store. If that decision hurt business, it was never apparent. By 1976, the café had expanded to 22 seats, and the staff had grown to 16. A larger location was badly needed. Larry's Butcher Shop, the 7000-square-foot neighborhood market where we would go when our supply of ripe avocados ran low, was just becoming vacant, and it was only two blocks away. A handshake deal from a local bank manager who was also a regular customer made the move possible.

The new store flourished. The restaurant grew to 72 seats, and the staff to around 80 people. Follow Your Heart had rapidly become one of the most successful independent natural food stores in the country. By 1982, a second store was opened in Santa Barbara, California. This store was later sold in 1997.

The four original founders ended their partnership in 1985, with Michael and Spencer leaving to pursue other interests. Bob and Paul as sole owners continue to be active in the business.

Over the years, many individuals have made contributions to Follow Your Heart: In the more than three decades of its existence, thousands of people have worked there. A handful—the core staff—have chosen to stay and make a career of "The Heart," and have been responsible for carrying the flame of that original idea and philosophy into the present. They are the "Heart of the Heart." Occasionally, people make the comment that Follow Your Heart is an "oasis." To the extent that this is true, it is indeed the legacy of those individuals who, through their work at Follow Your Heart, have dedicated themselves to that promise—to change the world.

Why Buy Organic?

I wish I could just write a cookbook and not have to discuss where to go to buy your food, but I can't. I wish we could go into a market anywhere and purchase food that is highly nutritious, grown in time-honored, proven ways without the use of pesticides, herbicides, fungicides, and artificial fertilizers. Instead, I'm compelled to tell you why I choose to buy and use organic foods whenever I can.

Remember when "the environment" seemed like something out there, far away, and miraculously forgiving? The attitude was, "Yeah, yeah, I know the environment's in trouble, but how does that affect me?" Now many more people realize it is close to home. The environment is us.

If you're not eating organically, you are shortchanging your health, your environment, and your taste buds. A lot is at stake from such simple acts as buying and eating groceries.

Buying organic food is good for our environment

Organic farming:

Protects our groundwater, which is currently being polluted by nitrate fertilizers and pesticides

Protects farmers and farmworkers from being exposed to pesticides and herbicides (Farmworkers have a high rate of certain kinds of cancers linked to chemical exposure. If you or your loved ones had these jobs, wouldn't you want protection from these chemicals?)

Creates healthy soil and prevents soil erosion (a big problem in commercial agriculture) by diversifying and rotating crops

Supports small farmers, a rapidly disappearing breed

I love the fact that in my community in Santa Barbara, small organic farms still coexist with residential neighborhoods. Stopping at a farm stand or the local farmer's market to pick up fresh produce is truly one of life's healthy pleasures.

Organic means culinary excellence

From a culinary standpoint, organic often tastes better. Soil that is cultivated and enriched by organic methods is nutrient rich, and it imparts this to the foods that are growing in it. Commercially farmed soil is often "tired": overused and undernourished. Often synthetic fertilizers have been added to replace what cultivation has taken out of the soil, but not in the same rich and delicate balance that nature or organic methods supply. Organic farmers also tend to plant unusual varieties of vegetables and fruits, which is great fun to add to your cooking experience. Older varieties of tomatoes, called "heirloom," come in an array of colors and delicious flavors. I'm partial to unusual squashes, small white eggplants, long Armenian cucumbers, and perfectly ripe apricots. A trip to the farmer's market gives me delicious raw materials with which to work.

Given these benefits, why wouldn't everybody buy organic? Many just don't know enough about it yet: Please tell them. It's convenient to shop at supermarkets. Sunday night you'll see those shopping carts, roaming the aisles of the frozen food section, being loaded up for the week. We're often short on time, and increasingly, short on basic cooking skills. But it's worth it to take the time to seek out organic foods.

Many are concerned about the extra costs at natural food stores. Organic foods can be more expensive, yet eating a vegetarian diet is often less expensive, so that's a plus. I figure that while I often pay more for my food, I pay less on medical bills. There are wiser ways to shop—the more you cook your own whole foods, the less you'll spend on packaged and highly refined products, which are more expensive and provide lower quality nutrition. Packaged products do save time and are helpful on those days when you have less time to cook. Look for items that are minimally processed, such as those that natural food stores carry. Canned beans and good whole grain breads, for example, are premade foods that won't compromise health.

Many supermarkets now carry some organic produce. Unfortunately it often looks terrible, because they don't sell that much of it. So shoppers get the idea that organic foods don't look as good and probably don't taste as good, when the problem isn't that they're organic—the problem is that they aren't fresh. Shopping at a natural food market like Follow Your Heart, which specializes in organic produce, means a higher turnover rate and much fresher food. And remember your farmer's markets and local produce stands.

The Scoop on Genetically Modified Foods

What are genetically modified foods, anyway?

They are foods both plant and animal, in which the gene structure has been altered by genetic engineering. Typically, a gene from a plant or animal is inserted into another organism for the purpose of adding a trait not normally found in that organism. For example, a specific gene from a flounder one that allows the flounder to thrive in a cold climate, might be inserted into a tomato to allow the tomato to survive colder growing temperatures.

Sounds interesting, except that flounders and tomatoes don't normally mate and marry. The idea of trans-species modification raises ethical, environmental, and health concerns. This kind of thing hasn't been done before; we're playing God and Goddess. Plant-breeding techniques have evolved over thousands of years as farmers have saved and selected seeds; more specific plant-breeding techniques have been developed in the last few hundred years, with Gregor Mendel* and Luther Burbank** leading the way. But it is a lengthy process, with built-in boundaries, and nothing like the kind of gene splicing that occurs with genetically modified foods.

Who is behind the movement to genetically alter foods?

Chiefly, multinational chemical companies. Since 1996, Monsanto has spent literally billions of dollars purchasing seed companies, and DuPont recently purchased Pioneer Hi-Bred. They both have a major stake in the world's seed companies. Other large companies, many of which are also multinational, involved in the agro-tech/seed business are AgrEvo (Germany), Novartis (Switzerland), Zeneca (UK), and Rhone-Poulenc (France).

What are major chemical companies doing in the seed business?

The chemical companies already make pesticides, and when the pesticides are used in conjunction with genetically modified seeds, they've created a package that is attractive to farmers, and a big money maker for the seed/chemical companies.

But letting genetically engineered seeds loose on the world could be a major Pandora's box. For thousands of years, farmers have saved their own seed for crop production, or at least had the option to do so. Some genetically modified seeds have a "terminator" gene, which keeps the plant from reproducing. This keeps farmers coming back to the large corporations for seeds every year, as is already true with hybrid seeds.*** But some of these "terminator" plants have bred with other non–genetically modified plants, hopping their fields, as plants and seeds tend to do. How will this terminator gene affect other crops? It is still too soon to tell. †

*Gregor Mendel, 1822–1884, Austrian monk and botanist whose plant research helped advance theories of genetic inheritance [Mendel's law].
**Luther Burbank, 1849–1926, U.S. horticulturalist and plant breeder.
***Since hybrids are a cross between different plant varieties, their offspring (seed) produce random mixtures of characteristics, not the parent plant.
†From Economic Impacts of Genetically Modified Crops on the Agri-Food Sector, Appendix A, Profiles of the Leading Agri-Biotech Firms: Internet, http://europa.eu.int/comm/agriculture/puli/gmo/fullrep/appen.htm.

Lab tests at Cornell University show that genetically engineered corn pollen, when ingested by Monarch butterfly larvae, can kill the larvae.* Might more of the insect kingdom be affected by genetically engineered crops? And what will happen if pests become resistant to pesticides in genetically modified crops? Will "super-pests" develop?

Let's look at a human health issue. So far, genetic scientists are trying to keep common allergenic foods out of genetically engineered crops. Nuts are a major cause of food allergies. During testing of genetically engineered foods, a gene from a Brazil nut was inserted into soybeans to see if people who were allergic to Brazil nuts would react to the beans. Most had positive allergic reactions. The company stopped using this gene.

But genetically engineered foods aren't labeled, and what if a person is allergic to an uncommon food? They would have no way of knowing if a food contains an altered gene, let alone a gene from a plant or animal they're allergic to. And would a vegetarian want to eat a tomato with flounder genes inserted into it?

The FDA has deemed genetically engineered foods safe to eat. But there isn't a strong regulatory system in place for these foods. The USDA, the FDA, and the EPA regulate different aspects of food production. According to an article in *Consumer Reports*, "No agency has taken responsibility for assessing the genetically engineered food with the pesticide in it. And the regulatory process is largely run on the honor system …. Companies that in the past have met performance standards are required to certify in a note to the USDA only that they will take the expected safety precautions."

At the present time, buying organic is the best way to ensure that your foods are not genetically modified, since no labeling is required in the United States.** Knowing the local farmer who produces your food is another great way to shop.

The FDA has approved some genetically engineered foods for sale. But are they safe enough? This rapidly growing technology has already changed the way America eats. If you're not buying organic, you are buying some genetically engineered foods. In 2003, 81 percent of the soybeans and 40 percent of the corn

*Consumer Reports, Sept. 1999, pg. 45, in reference to study in the journal *Nature*.
**There is concern in the organic foods industry that because of the way foods are processed, genetically engineered foods are mixed into organic foods. Organic corn and genetically engineered corn, for example, might be housed in the same storage containers and refined at the same mill.

crop were genetically engineered. The other large genetically engineered crop is cotton. In 2002, 71 percent of the U.S. cotton crop was genetically engineered, and cottonseed oil is in many processed foods including crackers and salad dressings. Besides these "big four," eight other crops have been approved for genetically engineered: potatoes, some squash, papayas, tomatoes, sugarbeets, rice, flax, and radicchio. Fortunately, most of these are not yet in production.*

Certified organic farming has all the tools to feed people in a non-risky way. But the chemical companies need to sell their products: genetically engineered seeds, artificial fertilizers, and pesticides. Agri-business is big business. Organic farming is not.

Unless, of course, consumers make it so.

*Refer to www.geo-pie.cornell.edu. The article referenced appears on the internet through the Genetically Engineered Organisms: Public Issues Education Project at Cornell University. The article is entitled, "Am I Eating GE soybeans?"

Appetizers and Beverages

Ah, polenta. It forms the base for the scrumptious flavor (and vibrant color) of these moist corn "hearts," topped with melted goat cheese and roasted peppers. Adapted from Viana La Place's book, *Panini*, this is especially beautiful served at a heartfelt occasion—such as a Valentine's Day feast.

Amore di Polenta

$6^1/_2$ cups water

2 teaspoons sea salt

2 cups instant polenta

2 tablespoons extra-virgin olive oil + more for brushing on polenta

2 large red bell peppers

4 ounces creamy goat cheese or imported blue cheese, such as creamy Gorgonzola

Freshly ground black pepper (optional)

To prepare the polenta: In a large saucepan, bring water and salt to a boil. Remove pot from heat; pour the polenta in a thin stream into the water, beating with a whisk or wooden spoon. Return pot to the stove and cook for 5 to 6 minutes over medium heat, stirring constantly. When polenta is thick and begins to pull away from the sides of the saucepan, it's done. Remove from heat and let the polenta settle for 1 minute. Working quickly, pour polenta into an 11-by-17-inch jellyroll pan, spreading with a spatula so mixture is smooth and level. (Dipping the spatula in water frequently keeps it from sticking.) Cool to room temperature (you can do this a day or two ahead of time; if so, allow to cool, then refrigerate, tightly covered).

While polenta is cooling, roast the peppers (see instructions, page 9).*

Cut open the roasted peppers. Remove seeds and stems. Cut peppers into long thin strips—you'll need about 18 strips from each pepper. Set aside.

Using a cookie cutter, cut polenta into about 36 small hearts. (The number is approximate—I used a heart about $2^1/_4$ inches wide by $2^1/_2$ inches long.) Save the scraps for another use.**

*If you don't have a gas stove, roast peppers under a hot broiler. Turn frequently until blackened all over, and proceed as above.
**The leftover polenta scraps are great for breakfast. Sauté them in a little butter or olive oil, and top with maple syrup, sorghum molasses, or jalapeño jelly. Serve warm.

Preheat the broiler. Brush both sides of polenta hearts lightly with oil, and arrange on 2 baking sheets, leaving a little space between them. Place hearts under the broiler; broil until crisp on the outside and barely browned, about 5 minutes. Turn and brown other sides in the same manner.

Top each heart with a strip of red pepper formed into a circle. Using a teaspoon, fill the circles with a little of the cheese you're using, about $1/2$ teaspoon per heart. With the heat off, return polenta hearts to the oven (not under the broiler) for just a moment to warm and soften but not melt the cheese. Serve immediately.

MAKES APPROXIMATELY 36 APPETIZER SERVINGS

Simple though it is, this recipe represents a breakthrough in the world of vegan recipes. Follow Your Heart has worked hard to create an all-vegetarian soy-based "cheese" that melts. It fooled some finicky eaters at my house, who thought it was dairy cheese.

"Cheesy" Garlic Bread

$1/2$ cup Vegenaise or eggless mayonnaise

1 cup shredded Vegan Gourmet Cheddar or Nacho Cheese Alternative* (beware—other brands don't melt)

1 cup thinly sliced green onions, both white and green parts, or $1/3$ cup fresh chives

2 cloves garlic, minced

1 baguette (about 20 inches), halved lengthwise, or 10 regular slices bread

$1/3$ cup minced fresh parsley, optional

Mix Vegenaise, cheese alternative, onions, and garlic. Spread on bread halves. Sprinkle with parsley if desired. Bake at 400°F for 5 to 10 minutes (depending on which bread you've used), or until cheese looks a little puffed and bread is beginning to brown. Cut into slices.

MAKES 8–12 SERVINGS

*Check Resources (page 195) for ordering information.

My friend Alessandro (Alex) makes the best bruschetta. He uses fresh ingredients: extra-virgin olive oil, red ripe tomatoes, fragrant herbs, and crispy ciabatta. Being Italian doesn't hurt either.

One summer my family had the good fortune to host a visiting Italian family for dinner. Nino is a third generation Tuscan olive grower, and his California-born wife, Lynn, and Italian-born daughters all help in the family business. We invited Alex and his family to this party, thinking he would love to have other Italians to talk to.

And he did. Everyone instantly loved each other. It was one of those August evenings you wish would never end. Conversations filled the air, which was also perfumed with the aroma of freshly chopped garlic and herbs.

Italians have this quality test they do when they open a bottle of olive oil. They rub a few drops in the palms of their hands until the oil is warm and fragrant, then they sniff, deeply. Needless to say, L'Arrigo, Nino and Lynn's oil, passed all tests.

Alex's Bruschetta

1 long loaf ciabatta (a flat, crunchy Italian bread), cut in $3/4$-inch-thick slices

2 large cloves garlic, sliced in half lengthwise

4 large tomatoes, cored and finely diced

$1/4$ cup chopped fresh basil

1 teaspoon finely chopped fresh oregano

Sea salt

Freshly ground black pepper

$1/4$ to $1/2$ cup best-quality extra-virgin olive oil

Preheat oven to 300°F. Place bread slices on ungreased baking sheets and toast just until slightly golden, 10 to 15 minutes. Remove from oven and set aside. When cool, rub toast slices with cut garlic.

Combine tomatoes, basil, and oregano. Taste and add salt and pepper to your liking. Set aside, but don't refrigerate—you can keep this for a couple of hours, covered, at room temperature, but it's better to serve right away.

Arrange bread slices on a large platter. Drizzle on a little oil, then spoon the tomato mixture over, and serve immediately.

Is there a better way to begin an elegant evening? Crisp, slightly bitter endive spears are filled with a little Roquefort cheese, sprinkled with roasted walnuts, and drizzled with vinaigrette. And don't be turned off by endive's bitter reputation: You'll also taste a contrasting sweet flavor, similar to some lettuces. (Please see Glossary, page 187, for more on Belgian endive and the chicory family.)

Endive with Roquefort and Walnuts

VINAIGRETTE

1/4 cup red wine vinegar

1/2 teaspoon Dijon mustard

1/2 teaspoon sea salt

1/8 teaspoon freshly ground black pepper

3/4 cup olive or walnut oil (but not toasted walnut oil) or mixture of the two

1/2 cup chopped walnuts

2 heads Belgian endive (look for short heads, tightly packed, and very fresh)

2 ounces Roquefort cheese

To make vinaigrette: Place vinegar, mustard, salt, and pepper in a small jar. Cover and shake well. Add the oil and shake well again, until dressing is creamy. Set aside. Shake well again before using. (You'll probably only need about half of the dressing. Save the rest for another salad.)

Place walnuts in a small, heavy skillet over medium heat, and cook, stirring often, just until walnuts are fragrant and golden, about 7 minutes. Set aside to cool.

variation If you'd like to serve this as finger food, keep endive leaves whole; wash and dry. Arrange on a platter in a sunburst pattern. Place a small piece of Roquefort on the base of each leaf, and garnish with walnut pieces. Drizzle a little dressing on each leaf and pass to serve.

MAKES 8 APPETIZER SERVINGS

One New Year's Eve several years ago, I found myself about to be divorced and in need of a good party. Giving one, that is. I pooled resources with a close friend, and we invited everyone we liked for an open house.

We agonized over the menu, and splurged on Italian sparkling wine neither of us could really afford. I borrowed a red velvet dress from another dear friend and we decorated my new home to the hilt with lights and greenery. Then we cooked for days.

We covered the table with appetizers and desserts, and let our friends bring more of the same. Friends and families came by all evening, several—even young children—making it all the way to midnight. Someone brought homemade beer. We danced to Cajun music. Now that was a party.

One of our most-loved appetizers that evening was these delightful filled corn cups, made in mini-muffin tins. Red salsa and fresh cilantro top the black bean filling, capped with a little snowy white sour cream.

Corn Cups filled with Black Beans

FILLING

1 tablespoon olive oil

1 large stalk celery, diced ($3/4$ cup)

1 small onion, finely chopped ($3/4$ cup)

1 large carrot, diced ($1/2$ cup)

One 15-ounce can black beans, including liquid

1 cup water

2 small tomatoes, preferably plum type, chopped (1 cup)

2 tablespoons chopped fresh cilantro

1 clove garlic, minced

$1/2$ teaspoon ground cumin

$1/4$ teaspoon chili powder

Tamari soy sauce

Dash of cayenne

CORN CUPS

8 tablespoons (1 stick) unsalted butter, at room temperature

2 ounces mild creamy goat cheese, at room temperature

1 cup cornmeal, the grainy kind used for making polenta

$^1/_2$ cup unbleached all-purpose flour

$^1/_4$ teaspoon sea salt

GARNISHES (OPTIONAL)

Tomato salsa

Cilantro leaves

Yogurt or sour cream

In a 9-inch sauté pan, heat oil over medium heat, and add celery, onion, and carrot. Sauté, stirring occasionally, for 5 to 7 minutes, or until slightly browned and a little tender. Add the beans, water, tomatoes, cilantro, garlic, cumin, chili powder, and tamari and cayenne to taste. Bring to a boil; reduce heat to low and simmer, uncovered, stirring occasionally, for 1 hour, or until mixture is thick and the flavors are well blended. Remove from heat, cover and set aside.

Preheat oven to 350°F.

Using a wooden spoon or bamboo rice paddle, cream together butter and goat cheese until smooth. Add cornmeal, flour, and salt and when it gets too stiff to stir, continue mixing with your hands just until a smooth dough is formed. Roll dough into 24 one-inch balls, and press into 24 mini-muffin cups, keeping dough a uniform thickness and pressing dough just up to top of cups. Bake for 15 to 20 minutes, or until just pale brown at edges. Cool in pan set on a cooling rack.

To serve, gently remove corn cups from tins. Fill with warm bean mixture and top, as desired, with tomato salsa, chopped cilantro, and a small spoonful of plain yogurt or sour cream.

note Corn cups should not be filled more than 15 minutes ahead of serving, as they will become soggy. But both the corn cups and the beans can be prepared several hours or even a day ahead. Store both, tightly wrapped, in the refrigerator; let corn cups return to room temperature before serving and reheat bean mixture before filling corn cups.

MAKES 24 CUPS, OR ABOUT 8 APPETIZER SERVINGS

Eggplant is such a flexible vegetable. You can roll it, stuff it, cut it into cubes, and sauté it—and it is delicious every way you try it.

This is a deceptively simple appetizer, adapted from Michelle Huneven's recipe for the *LA Times* magazine. Try varying the goat cheeses and herbs for different flavors.

Rolled Eggplant Stuffed with Goat Cheese and Herbs

1/2 cup extra-virgin olive oil + extra for greasing pan

1 tablespoon balsamic vinegar

8 ounces creamy goat cheese, plain, garlic-herb, or roasted red pepper flavor*

One 1-pound eggplant, oblong rather than globular (not the skinny Japanese eggplants, though; just look for a longish regular eggplant)

1 large bunch fresh basil or other herb, such as chervil, cilantro, or a small bunch of arugula

Preheat oven to 350°F.

Mix together the oil and vinegar.

Place goat cheese in a small bowl. If it is very creamy, use as is; if a little stiff, add 1 or 2 tablespoons of the oil mixture and mix until creamy. Set aside.

Using a very sharp knife, such as a bread knife with serrated edge, slice the eggplant into thin rounds, about 1/4 inch thick (not so thin that they'll burn or fall apart). Brush both sides of eggplant with oil-vinegar mixture, arrange on oiled baking sheets, and bake for 20 to 30 minutes, or until slices are cooked through and a little browned, but not crisp (they should be tender enough to roll). You can turn slices over halfway through if you wish, but it may not be necessary. (Alternatively, you may grill the eggplant slices on a hot grill, 3 to 5

*Skyhill Farms in Napa, California, makes a delicious goat cheese flavored (and colored a delicate pink) with roasted red peppers. It's available at natural food stores and gourmet cheese shops, or make your own by blending roasted red peppers with plain goat cheese in a food processor.

minutes per side. If you use a grill, you'll need to double the olive oil–balsamic mixture and baste additionally during the grilling.) Set eggplant slices aside.

Remove herb leaves from stems; medium leaves work better than very large or very small ones, if you have a choice. Set aside.

To make a roll, place an eggplant slice before you on a plate or board. Put 2 herb leaves on eggplant, toward the bottom of the slice with tips pointing out the sides. Place 2 or more rounded teaspoons of goat cheese on herb leaves and roll up eggplant. The tips of the herb leaves should be sticking out each end. Rolls will be $3/4$ to 1 inch thick.

Cover rolls tightly with plastic wrap and chill for an hour or two before serving, so they'll be firm. You can serve them whole, or slice in half and stand them up, clustered on a plate, cut sides down. If cheese doesn't get too soft, serve them at room temperature.

MAKES ABOUT 30 PIECES

To roast your own red peppers and make fabulous seasoned goat cheese: Turn a gas burner on medium-high. Using long-handled tongs, place a whole pepper on the burner grate. Turn it every 3 or 4 minutes. You want the outside of the pepper to char until most of it is black. Do this quickly; overcooking the pepper makes it soggy, which you don't want. The pepper should be charred in about 10 minutes. (You can also char the pepper under a broiler or on a gas or charcoal grill, again turning it frequently until charred all over.) Remove pepper from stove. Wrap in a paper towel and place in a brown paper bag; roll top down to close. Allow it to sweat there for 10 minutes or so. When the pepper is cool enough to handle, remove from bag, and use the paper towel to rub off the charred skin. Underneath you'll have a beautiful roasted pepper. Discard seeds and stem, and puree the pepper in a food processor. Add as much of this as you'd like to your goat cheese, to taste.

The combination of the crispy, mild blossoms with the creamy herbed goat cheese, garnished with red ripe tomato sauce, is divine. If you could taste summer, this would be it.

Just where can you find squash blossoms? The best place is your own garden, or the garden of a friend. Next best is a farmer's market during the summer, or specialty produce stores.

You can use the blossoms of any edible summer squash. Picking them means a squash won't develop there, and that can be a good thing, given the number of excess zucchini many gardeners have by the end of the summer! The plant will just keep producing more.

Squash blossoms have a delicate flavor. They must be fresh—just picked is best; they won't keep well in the refrigerator for more than a day or two.

Squash Blossoms Stuffed with Goat Cheese

20 very fresh zucchini or other edible squash blossoms

8 ounces creamy mild goat cheese

Olive oil

Chopped fresh herbs: your choice of thyme, basil, mint, parsley, oregano, chervil, etc.

Minced or pressed garlic (optional)

2 large ripe tomatoes, finely chopped, saving the juice

Sea salt

Freshly ground black pepper

Inspect squash blossoms: Don't get them wet, but check inside for bugs and dirt. Open them *gently*—they are fragile; if dirty, brush with a soft pastry brush and remove any ladybugs or other critters. Set aside.

Mix goat cheese with 1 tablespoon oil and a little of the freshly chopped herbs of your choice; thyme is especially nice. Add 1 or 2 large cloves garlic if you want. Using a narrow teaspoon, place 2 to 3 teaspoons of goat cheese inside each squash blossom. Brush each blossom with a little oil and place on an oiled baking sheet. Set aside.

Mix together the tomatoes, including their juices, with a little oil, more fresh herbs, and salt, pepper, and garlic, if desired, to taste. Set aside; it will taste better if it marinates a little while, say an hour. Serve the sauce at room temperature.

Preheat the broiler. Broil the squash blossoms for 3 to 5 minutes, just until edges of blossoms are a little browned and crisp, and cheese is soft, just beginning to melt. Serve warm, topped with a tablespoon or two of the tomato sauce.

MAKES 6 TO 8 APPETIZER SERVINGS

Spring rolls don't always have to be fried. Here the rice wrappers are moistened until tender, filled with vegetables and noodles, then rolled. The plump spring rolls are heated briefly in the oven before serving. Heating serves two purposes—to warm the appetizer and also to shrink the rice wrappers around the filling, making them easier to serve.

A sweet dipping sauce such as plum is ideal for these. I've found both light and dark plum sauces in natural food stores—one was Thai, the other Chinese. These are also good with a simple Ginger Dipping Sauce: Mix $^1/_4$ cup of your favorite soy sauce or tamari soy sauce with about $^1/_2$ teaspoon fresh ginger juice. To make ginger juice, grate fresh ginger, and press it through a fine sieve or squeeze it in your hand to extrude the ginger juice.

Spring Rolls

1 ounce fine bean thread noodles* (vermicelli), uncooked

2 tablespoons olive oil + extra for greasing pan

$^1/_4$ cup chopped green onions

2 cloves garlic, minced

1$^1/_2$ teaspoons minced peeled fresh ginger

1 teaspoon minced fresh basil

$^1/_2$ teaspoon minced or finely grated lemon peel (yellow part of skin only)

1 cup finely chopped Chinese or Napa cabbage

One 8-ounce can whole water chestnuts, sliced into thin sticks

4 ounces fresh shiitake mushrooms, thinly sliced

4 ounces seasoned (spicy, if desired) tofu, cut into thin matchsticks about 1$^1/_2$ inches long (optional, available in the refrigerated section of natural food stores)

About 1$^1/_2$ teaspoons hoisin** sauce or tamari soy sauce

*Bean thread noodles are also called glass noodles because they are clear when cooked. They're made of mung beans, not flour, and are available at Asian groceries and some supermarkets.
**Hoisin sauce is a sweet and salty Chinese sauce, available at Asian groceries, some supermarkets, and natural food stores. Try to find one without preservatives or MSG.

Five or Six 8½-inch rice paper or spring roll wrappers,* available at Asian groceries

Prepared plum sauce or Ginger Dipping Sauce (see page 12) as accompaniment

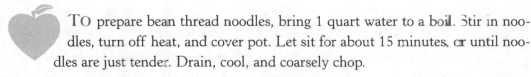

TO prepare bean thread noodles, bring 1 quart water to a boil. Stir in noodles, turn off heat, and cover pot. Let sit for about 15 minutes, or until noodles are just tender. Drain, cool, and coarsely chop.

Meanwhile, in a large skillet over medium heat, place oil. When oil is hot, but not smoking, add onions, garlic, ginger, basil, and lemon peel and stir for about 10 seconds. Add the cabbage, water chestnuts, and mushrooms and sauté for 2 or 3 minutes, or until cabbage and mushrooms are slightly wilted. Turn off heat, and stir in the noodles and tofu, if using. Season with the hoisin sauce. Allow to cool.

Fill a 9-inch pie plate or similar pan with about ½ inch of room temperature water. Slide in a couple of rice wrappers at a time, and let them soak for 2 or 3 minutes, completely immersed, until they are tender. Carefully remove from water and pat dry on clean kitchen towels. Put a couple more in to soak while you make the rolls.

It's just like filling a burrito: Place about ⅓ cup of the filling mixture in the center of the softened rice wrapper. Spread the filling before you into a rectangle about 2 inches wide and 4 inches long. Fold the short ends (top and bottom) over the filling; then fold the left side over the filling, and keep rolling over the right to make a neat package. Place on a platter seam side down. Continue until filling is used up. (If making ahead of time, cover tightly with plastic wrap and refrigerate for up to 2 hours.)

To serve: Preheat oven to 325°F. Place spring rolls, uncovered, on a lightly oiled baking sheet. Bake for about 7 minutes, or until wrappers tighten and spring rolls are heated through. Cut in half with a serrated knife. Serve immediately with plum sauce or Ginger Dipping Sauce.

MAKES 5 OR 6 LARGE SPRING ROLLS, OR ABOUT 4 APPETIZER SERVINGS

*Rice paper or spring roll wrappers look like translucent tortillas. They also come in a smaller 6-inch diameter, which you can use if you want to make smaller rolls and more of them, but the larger ones are easier to work with.

id Elizabethans love artichokes? Can't you just picture Shakespeare strolling the streets of London, artichoke in hand, discarding leaves carelessly and with a sonnet on his tongue?

These were inspired by the colossal artichokes served at southern California's Renaissance Faire, that springtime festival where vendors and participants dress as bawdy Elizabethans and eat sumptuous servings of messy food.

These artichokes are so flavorful they really don't need a dipping sauce. But if you must guild the lily, melted butter is always great. At the restaurant, we like to add crushed garlic to Vegenaise (see Glossary, page 187) for a garlic dip, and sometimes we include finely chopped basil as well.

Steamed Herbed Artichokes

4 medium artichokes

$^1/_2$ lemon

1 small onion, finely chopped

4 cloves garlic, crushed

1 tablespoon extra-virgin olive oil

6 cloves

2 bay leaves

1 teaspoon dried basil

1 teaspoon dried oregano

Remove stems and small bottom leaves from artichokes and with scissors, cut sharp leaf tips. Rub cut parts with the lemon half to prevent darkening. Add onion, garlic, oil, cloves, bay leaves, basil, and oregano to a large cooking pot (4 $^1/_2$ to 5 quarts). Place steamer tray on top of mixture; fill pot with water to approximately 1 inch above steamer tray. Arrange artichokes, tops down, on steamer tray. (Immersing them partly in water gives them a stronger herb flavor.) Cover, bring to a boil, reduce heat to simmer, and steam for 40 minutes, or until a fork can be easily inserted in base of artichokes. Serve warm or at room temperature.

Vegetarian chopped liver! Once this is baked, it's hard to believe it's vegetarian: a rich, flavorful, meaty-looking spread that's great on crackers or toast. Spread it while warm; it firms up when cool and is easy to slice, and then it makes a delicious filling for sandwiches.

Vegetable and Walnut Pâté

8 ounces green beans, fresh or frozen (1 1/2 cups)

4 ounces shelled peas, fresh or frozen (3/4 cup)

1 medium yellow onion, chopped (1 1/3 cups)

1 1/2 tablespoons safflower oil + extra for greasing pan

1 cup walnut pieces

1/3 cup tahini

4 teaspoons freshly squeezed lemon juice

2 cloves garlic, chopped

1 teaspoon balsamic vinegar

1 teaspoon sea salt

1/2 teaspoon freshly ground black pepper

1/2 teaspoon tamari soy sauce

1 1/2 teaspoons Ener-G Egg Replacer powder

2 tablespoons water

Preheat oven to 350°F.

Steam beans until just tender, about 7 minutes. If using fresh peas, steam until they are tender, 3 to 4 minutes. If using frozen peas, rinse under hot water to thaw. (Both beans and peas should be bright green after steaming or thawing—do not overcook.) Sauté onion with the oil in a medium sauté pan on low heat for about 20 minutes, stirring occasionally, until onions are fragrant, brown, and caramelized. In a nonstick pan, toast the walnuts over low heat, stirring often, until they are nicely browned and fragrant, about 10 minutes.

In a food processor container, place the cooked beans and peas, sautéed onions, toasted walnuts, tahini, lemon juice, garlic, vinegar, salt, pepper, and tamari, and process until smooth, about 20 seconds. Whisk together the egg replacer powder and water for about 2 minutes, until mixture is quite foamy. Add this to the mixture in food processor and process for just a couple of seconds, just until evenly mixed.

Pour mixture into an oiled loaf pan and bake for about 40 minutes, or until pâté has risen a little, is firm to the touch, and is slightly brown. Cool and serve at room temperature.

MAKES ABOUT 20 APPETIZER SERVINGS

Who invented the smoothie? I don't really know, but I imagine that it began in California. Maybe surfers brought the idea back from Mexico, where *licuados* are a popular drink made of milk or yogurt mixed with fruit and fruit juices.

It's a great way to start the day when I'm in a hurry. When my kids don't feel like a real breakfast, I make them one of these, with protein powder.

Fruit smoothie

1 banana, fresh or frozen, cut into large pieces

A few strawberries, peaches, or other soft fruit

$1/2$ to 1 cup juice, milk, or yogurt (pineapple and berry juices are especially good)

Dash of honey (optional)

2 or 3 ice cubes, or a few tablespoons water*

1 or 2 scoops protein powder** (optional)

Put the banana, fruit, juice, and honey, if using, into a blender container. Blend until smooth. Add ice and protein powder, if you are using. Blend until cubes are completely ground up. Pour and serve.

variation Other frozen fruits are nice to keep on hand for smoothies. Besides bananas, I've used frozen pineapple, raspberries, mangoes, peaches, and strawberries. So if you've got a surplus of ripe fruit on hand, cut it into small pieces and freeze it.

MAKES ONE 10- TO 12-OUNCE SMOOTHIE

*If you use frozen fruit, you don't really need ice. Use a little water instead.
**I use an organic, vanilla-flavored, rice protein powder. It's a little grainy for some people, though. Soy and whey protein powders are smoother; use one that you like. (Watch out for sugar and other additives.)

erved on a sultry summer day, this traditional Mexican beverage, called *jamaica* in Spanish (pronounced hamy-i-ka), is extremely refreshing, magenta in color, and slightly sour. The dried hibiscus flowers are steeped in boiling water and honey, then the liquid is strained and cooled.

Hibiscus flowers are available at natural food stores, herb stores, and Mexican markets.

Hibiscus Cooler

8 cups water

1/2 cup dried hibiscus flowers, also called *jamaica*

1/3 cup mild honey

Bring 4 cups water to a boil. Pour over hibiscus flowers and honey in a large bowl. Let steep for at least 1, but preferably several hours, covered. Strain into a pitcher, add remaining 4 cups water, and chill. Serve over ice.

MAKES 2 QUARTS, OR ABOUT 4 SERVINGS

Milkshakes 101

Follow Your Heart is famous for its tasty shakes. It was the boysenberry–apple juice shake that kept me coming to the lunch counter with my high-school girlfriends. That and the "Special," a vegetarian variation on a BLT (soy bacobits, melted cheddar, tomato, red onions, and sprouts on whole wheat). Of course, those young men working behind the counter were fascinating, too.

One of our secrets is an old-fashioned, soda fountain–style Hamilton Beach shake mixer, which most people don't have at home (although home versions are available). But a blender works well, too; just blend briefly to keep the shake really thick.

Our other secret is in the ice cream, or rather, the ice milk. At the restaurant, we use a honey ice milk, which gives a slushy texture, not too rich. Unfortunately this is no longer easily available (it must be ordered in a large quantity). Instead, use a quality vanilla ice cream.

You can also make delicious shakes by substituting soy ice cream or rice ice cream for the regular thing. Brands we've used successfully are Rice Dream frozen dessert (vanilla) and Soy Delicious organic frozen dessert (also vanilla). The Soy Delicious is milder tasting. Find a brand and flavor you like and experiment—I suspect many other companies will jump on the alternative milk bandwagon and products will just get better and more available.

You never know where a banana shake will lead. During his high school days, our own Bob Goldberg lived for the banana shakes at DQ (Dairy Queen) in his hometown, Chicago. Alas, he moved away, and no other shake could match it.

Years later, Bob wandered into Johnny Weismuller's American Natural Foods in Canoga Park, California, and found a banana shake on the menu. He sat down at the counter, ordered, sipped, and his life was forever changed. First he became a regular at that counter, then a partner in the business (which was sold and renamed Follow Your Heart), and 35 years later, he's still there.

There are reasons why a good banana shake is not easy to find. The banana must be properly ripe: just tender, with a few brown freckles on its skin. Too firm and it's astringent; too soft, and it's fermented. It should peel very easily but not be squishy or brown. There you go. I've given you our trade secret.

Banana shake

¹/₂ large ripe banana

Two 2-ounce scoops vanilla ice cream, vanilla Rice Dream frozen dessert, or vanilla Soy Delicious frozen dessert, very firmly frozen

¹/₂ cup milk or soymilk

A few drops vanilla extract

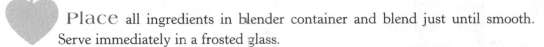 Place all ingredients in blender container and blend just until smooth. Serve immediately in a frosted glass.

variation Banana-Chocolate (or Carob) Shake **For a luscious alternative, make shake as above, only add 1¹/₂ teaspoons cocoa or roasted carob powder to the mixture, and omit the vanilla.**

MAKES ONE 10-OUNCE SHAKE

Downright refreshing and close to addictive. This shake tastes like a cold, creamy peppermint pattie.

Carob or Chocolate Chip Mint Shake

Four to five 2-ounce scoops of vanilla ice cream, very firmly frozen

3/4 cup milk or soymilk

4 drops mint extract

2 heaping tablespoons carob chips or malt-sweetened chocolate chips

 In a blender container, place ice cream, milk, and mint extract. Blend just a few seconds at medium speed, until smooth. Add carob chips and blend briefly again a few seconds (don't grind them up too much—keep them fairly chunky). Serve immediately.

MAKES TWO 8-OUNCE SHAKES

Fruity fresh, shockingly pink, smooth and creamy. The strawberry-apple juice intensifies the berry flavor.

Fresh Strawberry Shake

6 medium strawberries

1/3 cup strawberry-apple juice

Two (heaping) 2-ounce scoops vanilla ice cream, such as Soy Delicious vanilla frozen dessert or regular dairy vanilla ice cream, very firmly frozen

Mix all the ingredients in blender container just until smooth.

variation Strawberry and Banana Shake **Add one-half of a large banana for a really fruity treat.**

MAKES ONE 8-OUNCE SHAKE

O oh, this one tastes decadent. Rich, creamy, and oh so simple. Add half of a banana for an extra treat, and memories of childhood flavors.

Peanut Butter Shake

Four 2-ounce scoops vanilla ice cream, very firmly frozen

About $2/3$ cup milk

$1/4$ cup unsalted peanut butter

 Place ice cream, milk, and peanut butter in blender container. Blend just until smooth. Serve immediately.

MAKES TWO 8-OUNCE SHAKES

Breads and Breakfasts

When I married my first husband in 1980, cinnamon rolls similar to these served as the wedding cake, stacked in tiers and topped with the traditional bride and groom. The wedding was in the morning, so these made more sense than a traditional wedding cake.

These currant-pecan cinnamon rolls are tender and scrumptious. Concentrated fruit juice is the unusual sweetener. They're sweet and lusciously cinnamony, but the sweetness is subtle, not overpowering, as pastries can sometimes be. If you can't find this sweetener, check out the ordering information below, or substitute with maple syrup or honey.

This recipe can be easily doubled.

Cinnamon Rolls

4 teaspoons active dry yeast

1/4 cup lukewarm water

3 cups unbleached all-purpose flour + plus extra for kneading

1 3/4 cup whole wheat pastry flour

1/2 teaspoon ground cinnamon

1/4 teaspoon sea salt

8 tablespoons (1 stick) unsalted butter, melted

1 cup fresh honey-sweetened soymilk (in refrigerator section)

1/2 cup liquid mixed fruit concentrate sweetener (such as Mystic Lake Dairy brand,* available in refrigerator section at natural food stores), or substitute maple syrup or mild-flavored honey

Vegetable oil or butter for greasing pan

TOPPING

8 tablespoons (1 stick) unsalted butter, at room temperature

1/2 cup (liquid) fruit concentrate sweetener (see above) + additional tablespoon to brush on before baking

2 1/2 teaspoons ground cinnamon

*Mystic Lake Dairy makes the fruit juice concentrate sweetener we use in this recipe. If it's not available in your area, you can order it by phoning 425-868-2029, or go to their Web site, www.mysticlakedairy.com.

1 cup chopped pecans or walnuts

1 cup dried currants or raisins

 In a small bowl, combine yeast and water and stir to dissolve. Place in a warm place for a few minutes, until mixture starts to look bubbly.

If using electric mixer

Place both flours, cinnamon, and salt in bowl of mixer. Using paddle attachment, mix at low speed to combine well.

Combine butter with the soymilk and fruit concentrate. With mixer running at low speed, add butter mixture to the flour mixture, then add proofed yeast and water. When all is combined well, stop machine and change to dough hook attachment. At low speed, let machine knead dough for 10 to 12 minutes, or until dough is smooth and elastic. Add a small amount of additional flour if necessary; finished dough will be soft, but not sticky. (These directions apply to a KitchenAid mixer; if you're using another brand, you may have to adjust directions according to your manual.)

If mixing by hand

In a large bowl, stir together the flours, cinnamon, and salt.

Combine butter with the soymilk and fruit concentrate. Stir this into the flour mixture; add proofed yeast and water mixture and stir thoroughly. When all is combined well, turn out onto a floured board and knead 15 to 20 minutes, or until dough is smooth, soft, and elastic, but not sticky (add additional flour if necessary).

Proceed for both methods

Place dough in a large, oiled bowl covered with a damp towel, and let rise in a warm place until doubled in bulk, about 1 hour.

Meanwhile, prepare topping: With a handheld electric mixer, combine butter, fruit concentrate, and cinnamon, and mix until fluffy. (If you are doing this by hand, you'll have to beat softened butter very well with a spoon or whisk, then add fruit concentrate and cinnamon. It won't get as fluffy as mixer version.) Set aside.

Preheat oven to 350°F.

On a floured board, roll out dough into a large rectangle about 12 by 18 inches. Spread topping evenly across dough, all the way to the edges. Sprinkle on the nuts and currants, distributing them evenly out to the edges. Starting at one of the narrow sides, carefully roll dough into a log; press edge into log to seal. Using a sharp knife, slice into 2-inch-thick rounds. Place on an oiled baking sheet, about $^1/_2$ inch apart; cover with plastic wrap and let rise again in a warm place until doubled, about 30 minutes. Gently brush on 1 tablespoon of liquid sweetener evenly across tops of buns. Bake for 25 to 30 minutes, or until nicely browned. Serve warm.

MAKES 9 SERVINGS

This recipe was adapted from Myrtle Allen's *Cooking at Ballymaloe House*, a lovely Irish cookbook. It is relatively low in fat as scones go, using buttermilk in place of the usual cream (which also gives a luscious flavor) and a small amount of butter. Baking soda reacts with the buttermilk, causing the scones to rise beautifully.

Irish Buttermilk Scones

$1^1/2$ cups unbleached all-purpose flour + plus extra for kneading

$1/2$ cup whole wheat pastry flour

$1/2$ teaspoon baking soda

$1/4$ teaspoon sea salt

4 tablespoons ($1/2$ stick) unsalted butter, cold, cut in pieces

$1/2$ cup buttermilk

$1/4$ cup mild honey (should be very liquid; if necessary, warm to melt, then cool before adding to buttermilk)

Preheat oven to 400°F.

Sift together the flours, baking soda, and salt. With a pastry blender or 2 knives, cut in the butter until mixture resembles coarse meal. Stir together the buttermilk and honey; stir this mixture into the flour-butter mixture all at once, and mix with a spoon just until all ingredients are moistened and a dough forms (don't overmix).

Turn dough out onto a lightly floured surface and knead 4 or 5 times. Pat the dough into a $3/4$-inch-thick circle (about 7 inches in diameter), and cut it into 8 triangular wedges. Arrange 2 inches apart on an ungreased baking sheet. Bake for 12 to 14 minutes, or until well risen and tops are golden brown. Transfer immediately to a wire rack to cool. Serve warm, preferably, with jam, butter, and honey.

MAKES 8 SERVINGS

One day I received *The Quaker Oats Wholegrain Cookbook* in the mail. It was sent by my dad, who'd thoughtfully ordered copies for myself and my two sisters. This recipe was adapted from that cookbook, and has seen plenty of mileage over the years. It's great for breakfast or brunch, and is easy, fast, and fun to make.

Scottish Oat Scones

10 tablespoons (1 $^1/_4$ sticks) unsalted butter, melted, or $^1/_2$ cup safflower oil

$^1/_3$ cup milk or soymilk

$^1/_4$ cup mild honey

2 tablespoons water

1 $^1/_2$ teaspoons Ener-G Egg Replacer powder

1 $^1/_2$ cups sifted whole wheat pastry flour + plus extra for kneading

1 $^1/_4$ cups quick-cooking oats

1 tablespoon baking powder

1 teaspoon cream of tartar

$^1/_2$ teaspoon sea salt

$^1/_2$ cup raisins or currants

Vegetable oil for greasing pan

Preheat oven to 425°F.

In a small bowl, combine butter, milk, honey, water, and egg replacer (if honey is very thick, dissolve it in the melted butter first). In another bowl, combine flour, oats, baking powder, cream of tartar, and salt. Add liquid to dry ingredients, stirring just until dry ingredients are moistened. Stir in raisins. Shape dough to form a ball; pat out on a lightly floured surface to form an 8-inch circle. (Mixture may be very moist—if you let the circle sit for a few minutes it will begin to dry and become easier to handle.) Cut into 8 wedges. Carefully transfer the scones to an oiled baking sheet, arranging scones so there is about 1 inch between them. Bake for 12 to 15 minutes, or until a light golden brown. Serve warm at breakfast or brunch with butter, preserves, or honey, as desired.

MAKES 8 LARGE SCONES OR 12 TO 16 MINI-SCONES

These muffins are a favorite at our restaurant, where we make them jumbo sized. Here, the recipe is designed to be baked in a regular 12-cup muffin pan.

Olallieberries are a type of big, juicy blackberry, but you can use regular blackberries or raspberries, fresh or frozen.

Olallieberry Bran Muffins

1½ cups wheat bran

1½ cups sifted whole wheat pastry flour

1½ teaspoons baking powder

¾ teaspoon sea salt

1 cup soymilk

½ cup honey

⅓ cup unsulphured Barbados molasses or other light molasses (not blackstrap)

¼ cup safflower or canola oil

½ teaspoon vanilla extract

2¼ teaspoons Ener-G Egg Replacer powder

3 tablespoons water

1 cup olallieberries, raspberries, or blackberries, fresh or frozen (do not defrost frozen berries—they'll turn mushy if you do)

Preheat oven to 350°F. Fill a 12-cup (3 ounces each) muffin tin with paper liners. Stir together the bran, flour, baking powder, and salt. Set aside.

In a separate bowl, combine the soymilk, honey, molasses, oil, and vanilla, and mix thoroughly. With a wire whisk, beat the egg replacer powder into the water until foamy.

Stir combined dry ingredients into the soymilk mixture. Combine just until smooth; do not overbeat. Gently fold in the egg replacer mixture.

Spoon batter evenly into the muffin cups. Push 3 or 4 berries in each of the cups, letting 1 peek out of each. Bake for 25 to 30 minutes, until a tester inserted in the middle of one comes out clean. Let cool on wire racks.

MAKES 12 MUFFINS

Jewel-like pieces of cranberry make this a festive loaf. Serve it warm for breakfast with a little butter. Be sure to prepare the walnuts, cranberries, and orange peel ahead of time, so that once the batter is mixed you get it right into the oven. The baking powder and soda react rapidly with the liquid ingredients: The faster it begins baking, the better it will rise.

Cranberry Bread

1 cup mild honey

8 tablespoons (1 stick) unsalted butter + extra for greasing pan

$1/2$ cup freshly squeezed orange juice

$2^1/4$ cups sifted whole wheat pastry flour

$1/4$ teaspoon sea salt

$2^1/4$ teaspoons baking powder

1 teaspoon baking soda

$1^1/4$ teaspoons Ener-G Egg Replacer powder

3 tablespoons water

8 ounces fresh cranberries, finely chopped (2 cups chopped)

$1/2$ cup chopped walnuts

2 tablespoons freshly grated orange peel (orange part only)

Preheat oven to 350°F. Grease a $4^1/2$-by-$8^1/2$-inch loaf pan.

In a small saucepan, combine honey, butter, and orange juice. Heat gently just to melt butter and honey; set aside.

Combine flour and salt and set aside. In a separate small bowl, combine baking powder and baking soda and set aside. In another small bowl, whisk together egg replacer powder and water until frothy, and set aside.

Pour the melted butter mixture into a large heatproof bowl. Into this mixture whisk in the baking powder and baking soda mixture, then stir in the flour mixture about $1/2$ cup at a time, alternating with the egg replacer mixture. Do not overmix at this point; just stir a few times to mix. Gently fold in the cranberries, walnuts, and orange peel. Spoon mixture into the prepared loaf pan, and bake on center rack of oven for 55 to 60 minutes, or until a toothpick inserted in center of loaf comes out clean.

Place pan on rack to cool. Serve warm or at room temperature. After cooling, wrap in plastic bag to store. Wrapped, it will keep for several days at cool room temperature.

MAKES 10 TO 12 SERVINGS

I'm tempted to rename this Irish-American soda bread, because it strays from some of the traditional recipes. A friend from Ireland says that she would never use thyme in hers or baking powder or eggs, which the egg replacer is replacing! Still, this is so good, and it looks and tastes like Irish soda bread. It follows the traditional quick baking method, and has the deep cross cut into the loaf.

Fresh thyme delicately flavors this bread. And if you're of a mind with my friend Mary Murphy, leave out the thyme altogether. Add a handful of raisins instead.

Be certain that your baking powder and especially baking soda are very fresh—a well-risen, light Irish soda bread depends on the reaction of the soda and buttermilk, with help from the baking powder and egg replacer.

Irish Soda Bread

2 cups unbleached all-purpose flour + extra for kneading

1 cup whole wheat pastry flour

2 tablespoons maple sugar or unbleached cane sugar

$2^1/_2$ teaspoons baking powder

$^1/_2$ teaspoon baking soda

$^1/_2$ teaspoon sea salt

$^3/_4$ cup cultured buttermilk

2 tablespoons melted butter + extra for greasing pan

$1^1/_2$ teaspoons Ener-G Egg Replacer powder

2 tablespoons water

$1^1/_2$ teaspoons finely chopped fresh thyme leaves (discard stems)

Preheat oven to 425°F.

In a large bowl, stir together the flours, sugar, baking powder, baking soda, and salt until well combined. In a separate bowl, stir together the buttermilk and butter. Whisk the egg replacer powder into the water until very frothy; stir this gently into the buttermilk mixture, along with the thyme. Add liquid to dry ingredients and stir gently until a soft, moist dough is formed.

Fold dough over a couple of times, then turn out onto a lightly floured surface, and form into a large round disk about 7 inches in diameter. Using a sharp knife, cut a deep cross into the top of the dough, cutting the disk almost (but not quite) into quarters. Bake the bread on a buttered baking sheet, on middle rack of oven, for 15 minutes. Reduce heat to 350°F and bake for another 10 to 15 minutes, or until nicely browned and tester comes out clean. Cool on a rack.

MAKES 1 LARGE, ROUND LOAF

This makes a lot of cornbread. It keeps well for a couple of days at room temperature, covered. This is a bread you won't mind having around for snacks and it's delicious as a base for Roasted Eggplant, Leeks, and Italian Cheeses on Cornbread (page 91).

Moist Oatmeal Cornbread

$1/4$ cup + 2 tablespoons boiling water

1 cup ground oats (use rolled or quick oats, finely ground in food processor or blender to yield 1 cup)

$1/2$ cup fresh or frozen corn kernels

$1 1/4$ cup fresh honey soymilk

$3/4$ cup canola oil + extra for greasing pan

$1/2$ cup mild honey

1 tablespoon Ener-G Egg Replacer powder

$2 1/2$ cups fine yellow cornmeal, the type used for polenta

$1 1/2$ tablespoons baking powder

1 teaspoon sea salt

Preheat oven to 350°F.

In a small heatproof bowl, pour boiling water over ground oats and stir into a smooth paste. Let sit 5 minutes. Meanwhile, steam corn 5 minutes, or until just tender. Then place the oatmeal paste, corn, soymilk, oil, honey, and egg replacer powder in a blender container. Blend until smooth, about 10 seconds.

Combine cornmeal, baking powder, and salt and mix well. Pour liquids into cornmeal mixture, and quickly mix using just a few strokes. Pour into an oiled 9-by-13-by-1$1/2$-inch baking pan, and bake for 25 to 30 minutes, until cornbread is lightly browned, firm to the touch, and toothpick inserted in center comes out clean.

Cool in pan before cutting.

MAKES ABOUT 12 SERVINGS

Schiacciata* con l'Uva (Flatbread with Grapes) is a Tuscan treat made at harvest time in Italy. It looks like a pizza with grapes scattered across it, and in fact is made with pizza dough. This particular version was adapted from a recipe by Giuliano Bugialli, the Italian cookbook author.

The dough is prepared by making a well in the flour, pouring in the liquid ingredients, and stirring in just a little flour at a time. This is the same way fresh pasta dough is made. It's a great technique because you can easily control the amount of flour needed, which varies according to the moisture content of the flour and the weather conditions. This method also produces a very smooth dough.

Serve at breakfast, dessert, or as a late afternoon snack with an Italian cheese, such as Asiago or Parmigiano-Reggiano, and a glass of Chianti.

Schiacciata con l'Uva

SPONGE

4 teaspoons active dry yeast

1 1/4 cups lukewarm water

1 cup unbleached all-purpose flour

DOUGH

2 pounds seedless ruby red grapes or red wine or champagne grapes (Sangiorese grapes are preferred if you can find them)

1 cup maple sugar or unbleached cane sugar

1/2 teaspoon fennel seeds, lightly crushed in a mortar and pestle

1 cup whole wheat pastry flour

2 cups unbleached all-purpose flour

2 tablespoons extra-virgin olive oil + extra for greasing pan

1/4 teaspoon sea salt

Prepare sponge by dissolving yeast in water; gradually add flour and stir to dissolve lumps. Cover bowl with a towel and put in a warm place for 1 hour, or until sponge is doubled in bulk.

*Pronounced Skee-ah-cha-ta.

While sponge is rising, stem grapes and wash in cold water. Drain and pat with towels, until grapes are just a little damp, and place in a large bowl with the sugar and fennel seeds. Stir gently but well to coat grapes with sugar. Set aside.

Combine flours and mix well. Pour onto a large board, and arrange into a mound about 8 inches in diameter with a well in the middle. Pour half of the sponge into the well, along with the oil and salt and, with a wooden spoon, stir gently, incorporating a little of the flour from the mound as you stir. As mixture begins to thicken, add the rest of the sponge and continue to stir, bringing in more flour from rim of the well until most of the flour is incorporated. Then knead the dough, using more or less flour as necessary, until dough is smooth and elastic (about 5 minutes).

Oil a 14-inch pizza pan.

Divide dough in half. On a floured board, roll each piece into a 14-inch circle. Lay first circle on pizza pan. Distribute half of the grapes, and sprinkle sugar evenly across surface (bring grapes and sugar mixture almost out to the edges); cover with the other circle of dough, and seal edges of dough together. Distribute remaining grapes and sugar mixture evenly across the top surface.

Cover dough with a towel, and let rise in a warm place until schiacciata is doubled in size, about 1 hour.

Preheat oven to 375°F.

Bake schiacciata for about 50 minutes, or until it has a crispy, golden brown crust. Serve warm or at room temperature, cut into pizza wedges.

MAKES 8 LARGE SERVINGS

A variation of Schiacciata con l'Uva, using the same basic dough. Simple and savory with the flavor of fresh rosemary, it makes a wonderful appetizer or snack. Use this at the start of an autumn meal of Pasta e Ceci (page 102) and Easier Caesar salad (page 60). Finish with simple poached pears.

Schiacciata with Rosemary

1 recipe schiacciata dough (page 35)

4 tablespoons olive oil + plus extra for greasing pan

2 tablespoons fresh rosemary leaves

2 teaspoons kosher salt

Make dough as in Schiacciata con l'Uva (page 35), omitting topping. When it comes time to divide the dough in half, you can make this one of two ways:

For a very thin schiacciata, oil two 14-inch pizza pans or 2 large rectangular baking sheets. Divide dough in half and roll out dough quite thinly to fit pans. Drizzle with oil, sprinkle on the rosemary and salt; cover loosely with plastic wrap and let rise for about 1 hour, until doubled in bulk.

Preheat oven to 375°F.

Remove plastic wrap and bake for about 15 to 20 minutes, or until crisp on the bottom and lightly browned.

For a thicker schiacciata, oil one 14-inch pizza pan or large rectangular baking sheet. Divide dough in half, and roll out in two thin sheets to fit your pan. Place first circle of dough in pan; top with half of the olive oil and half of the rosemary. Top with second circle of dough, the remaining olive oil, rosemary, and all of the salt. Cover loosely with plastic wrap and let rise for about 1 hour, until doubled. Remove plastic wrap and bake for about 25 to 30 minutes, or until nicely browned.

MAKES 8 LARGE SERVINGS

Everybody's on the soy bandwagon these days because of those yummy phyto-estrogens and cancer-fighting isoflavones. Besides the health benefits, I've always loved adding soy flour to baked goods because of its nutty flavor, fine texture, and golden color. Soy is also high in protein. Blue cornmeal is a nice variation on the old yellow standard, and it tastes different, too—a little nuttier. This recipe can be halved successfully.

Blue Cornmeal Flapjacks

2 cups blue cornmeal

2 cups soy flour

2 teaspoons baking powder

1 teaspoon sea salt

1 teaspoon ground cinnamon

1 teaspoon baking soda

$3^{1}/_{3}$ cups fresh honey soymilk

4 teaspoons mild honey

1 tablespoon canola oil

2 tablespoons + 2 teaspoons Ener-G Egg Replacer powder

$^{1}/_{3}$ cup water + more as needed

2 cups fresh or frozen, thawed, corn kernels

 Stir cornmeal, flour, baking powder, salt, cinnamon, and baking soda together thoroughly. Set aside.

In a separate bowl, combine soymilk, honey, and oil. Set aside.

In a blender container, or in a small bowl and using a wire whisk, mix egg replacer powder with water until frothy. Stir into soymilk mixture.

Combine wet and dry ingredients, stirring just to mix. Fold in corn. Add water if necessary to obtain consistency of thick cream, possibly up to $^{1}/_{2}$ cup.

Heat an oiled griddle or skillet over medium-high heat. Cook pancakes, approximately 3 or 4 inches in diameter until large bubbles form. Flip and cook on other side several minutes, or until browned on that side and cooked through. Serve with butter and maple syrup, jam, or jalapeño jelly.

MAKES 6 SERVINGS

When Follow Your Heart decided to begin serving breakfast after years of being open only for lunch and dinner, we brought in my old friend and college roommate Stacy Wyman for several months to help with recipe development. Since making pancakes without eggs can be tricky, we made dozens of trials before settling on the recipes we use today. These popular buttermilk pancakes are the result.

Buttermilk Pancakes

1 cup sifted unbleached all-purpose flour

1 cup sifted brown rice flour

$^1/_3$ cup sifted whole wheat pastry flour

2 tablespoons Ener-G Egg Replacer powder

2 tablespoons wheat bran

2 tablespoons raw wheat germ, preferably fresh, vacuum packed

$1^1/_2$ teaspoons baking powder

1 teaspoon sea salt

1 teaspoon baking soda

$2^1/_2$ to 3 cups buttermilk

4 teaspoons safflower oil plus more for griddle

$2^1/_4$ teaspoons honey or brown rice syrup, very liquid (heat slightly if solid)

 In a large bowl, stir together thoroughly flours, egg replacer, wheat bran, wheat germ, baking powder, salt, and baking soda. Set aside.

In another large bowl, mix together $2^1/_2$ cups buttermilk, oil, and honey. Stir dry ingredients into buttermilk mixture, stirring just enough to combine. If mixture is too thick, add the additional buttermilk to the correct consistency, so that batter looks like heavy cream.

Heat a well-seasoned griddle, using very little or no safflower oil, on medium-high heat. Make pancakes about 4 inches in diameter; flip when bubbles form, and cook other side just until lightly browned and cooked through. Serve immediately with butter and jam or maple syrup. Top also with yogurt and fresh sliced fruit, if desired.

MAKES 4 SERVINGS

I served this breakfast dish to children who wouldn't eat eggy French toast because it was "too gross," and to children who liked regular French toast but who'd never had tofu, and both groups gave it their stamp of approval (cleaned their plates). If you choose to include a banana in the batter you'll be rewarded with a heavenly childhood flavor: fried bananas. It's subtle, yet ambrosial.

Cooking hints: This French toast is trickier to cook than one made with eggs. Use a heavy, well-seasoned pan or griddle, and make sure the surface is well oiled or use a good vegetable cooking spray, especially for the first few slices. If not, the batter has a habit of separating from the toast. If you've cooked a few slices and then the bread begins to stick, add a little more oil to the empty griddle, heat well, then begin with your next batch. Also, the 3-minute soaking time is important to the success of this recipe, so don't rush; it helps keep the bread from sticking.

You can make the batter ahead of time and refrigerate for 1 or 2 days.

Tofu French Toast

Vegetable oil for frying (such as safflower)

12 ounces fresh soft tofu

1^{1}/2 cups fresh honey soymilk (sold in refrigerator section)

3 tablespoons maple syrup

1 tablespoon ground cinnamon

1^{1}/2 teaspoons vanilla extract

^{1}/2 teaspoon turmeric

^{1}/4 teaspoon sea salt

1 ripe banana, peeled (optional)

1 loaf stale French bread (a large baguette), potato bread, or sourdough, sliced ^{3}/4 inch thick

Maple syrup, jam, and butter as accompaniments

Fresh berries (optional)

Preheat griddle or large, heavy frying pan (such as cast iron) over medium-high heat. Add a little oil. (Add more later as needed.)

Place tofu, soymilk, syrup, cinnamon, vanilla, turmeric, salt, and banana, if using, in a blender container and blend until smooth. Pour into a wide, shallow bowl. Soak slices of bread in batter for at least 3 minutes, turning to coat thoroughly.

Meanwhile, oil griddle generously and make sure oil is quite hot, but not smoking; add several slices of French toast. Cook first side until browned, about 2 minutes, lifting carefully while turning to keep the batter on the toast. Flip over and brown other side. Serve immediately with accompanying syrup, jam, butter, and fresh fruit.

MAKES 4 TO 6 SERVINGS

Bob's Breakfast got its inspiration when one of Follow Your Heart's owners visited Pasqual's Café in Santa Fe, New Mexico. This restaurant serves an egg dish called *Huevos Motuleños,* which means "eggs in the style of Motul," Motul being a village on Mexico's Yucatan peninsula. Corn tortillas are covered with black beans, eggs, red and green salsas, and topped with a sprinkling of crumbled white cheese.

Since we don't serve eggs at Follow Your Heart, we replaced the eggs with sautéed tofu and changed the name to *Huevos No Tenemos,* loosely translated as "We don't have eggs."

Unfortunately this attempt at a humorous rhyming play on words only works if you understand Spanish, so the name evolved into the more practical Bob's Breakfast. Whatever you call it, it's a delicious way to start the day.

Bob's Breakfast aka Huevos No Tenemos

1 tablespoon olive oil

$^1/_2$ cup finely chopped red onion

1 large clove garlic, minced

2 cups Basic Black Beans (page 73) or canned whole black beans, drained

$^1/_4$ cup water

$^1/_2$ teaspoon ground cumin

Sea salt (optional)

4 corn tortillas

TOFU

1 tablespoon olive oil

1 tablespoon unsalted butter

6 ounces firm fresh tofu, drained and cut into $^3/_4$-inch cubes

Sea salt

Freshly ground black pepper

Mild red salsa, such as Herdez

Mild green salsa (made from tomatillos), such as Herdez

2 or 3 tablespoons *queso seco,* a crumbly, salty, Mexican white cheese, or you can use feta cheese or a dry crumbly goat cheese

1 tablespoon chopped fresh cilantro

Preheat oven to 300°F.

Place a 10-inch skillet over medium heat. Add oil, and when hot but not smoking, add the onion. Sauté until golden and almost translucent, about 5 minutes, stirring often. Add garlic, and sauté another minute.

Add black beans, water, and cumin. Bring to a boil, then reduce heat and simmer, covered, for about 5 minutes. Remove cover. If beans are too liquid, continue cooking, uncovered, until beans are thick. Or if beans are too dry, add a little more water. Mash beans with a potato masher until they are somewhat creamy. Turn off heat. Add salt, if using, and adjust seasonings to taste. Keep beans covered and warm while you prepare tofu.

Wrap tortillas in foil and place in oven to warm.

In a small heavy skillet (I like cast iron for this), heat oil and butter together over medium heat. When hot, but before butter browns, add tofu. Stir often, trying to brown all sides of cubes for 5 to 8 minutes, or until tofu is golden. Remove from heat; add salt and pepper, to taste.

Arrange on each of 2 plates: 2 warm tortillas topped with the warm black beans, cubed tofu, arranged to look like mountains and the red and green salsas, drizzled over the tofu and beans (served side by side, so their distinct colors show). Top with the crumbled cheese and the fresh cilantro. Serve immediately.

MAKES 2 SERVINGS

Great breakfast potatoes are the sign of a great restaurant. These are baked, not fried, yet still golden and crisp. Serve alongside Scrambled Tofu (page 48) or with Tofu Benedict (page 49). When you prebake the potatoes, slightly underbaking them makes them more attractive in this dish, since they'll hold together better when sliced. However, any leftover baked potatoes will do.

Breakfast Potatoes

2 pounds red or russet potatoes or leftover baked potatoes

$3/4$ cup finely diced green pepper

$2/3$ cup diced yellow onion

2 tablespoons safflower oil + extra for greasing pan

2 tablespoons sliced pimento

2 large cloves garlic, minced

$1/2$ teaspoon sea salt

Freshly ground black pepper

Preheat oven to 400°F.

If using raw potatoes, bake for 40 to 60 minutes, depending on size, or until just tender. Cool slightly.

Cut cooled (or leftover) potatoes in quarters lengthwise, then slice crosswise approximately $3/8$ inch thick. Set aside.

Mix together green pepper, onion, oil, pimento, garlic, and salt and pepper to taste. Gently add the potatoes and stir just to mix. Arrange mixture in a well-oiled 9-by-13-inch baking dish, and bake uncovered, on lower rack of oven, for 45 minutes, or until nicely browned and crisp. Serve warm.

MAKES 4 SERVINGS

People don't want to talk about eating prunes for breakfast. But why not? They're tasty. A scrumptious topping for pancakes, cooked cereal, or plain yogurt, this compote is naturally sweet—it needs no added sweetener. Both apricots and prunes are high in vitamin A, as well as iron and potassium.

Be sure to buy unsulphured fruit if you can. Sulphur is used as a preservative and antioxidant; it keeps dried fruit from darkening, but is also an unnecessary additive. It can leave a burning sensation in the back of the throat and is considered by many to be a toxin. I prefer my dried fruits less colorful, but good for you. Unsulphured dried fruits are widely available at natural food stores and some farmer's markets.

Fruit Compote

1 cup (about 8 ounces) pitted dried unsulfured prunes

$^2/_3$ cup (2 ounces) dried unsulfured apricots

2 cups water

1 small cinnamon stick, about $2^1/_2$ inches long

Rinse fruit and check that it is free of stones. Combine all ingredients in a small saucepan; bring to a boil, reduce heat, and simmer, covered, for 5 minutes. Remove from heat and let cool. Discard cinnamon stick after mixture has cooled. Can be stored in refrigerator for about 1 week. Serve warm or at room temperature.

MAKES 4 SERVINGS

I love this unusual breakfast dish. When my friend Kathy Goldberg served this to my family for breakfast, I wasn't sure if my kids ate it because they were being polite or because they really liked it. But when I made it for dinner at home with plain brown rice, they devoured it.

The textures, the flavors, and the unusual combination of ingredients add up to a satisfying dish with Italian overtones, yet it contains Asian ingredients as well: tamari and toasted sesame oil. Vegetarian cooks have long been exploring the possibilities of tamari in everything from chili to sauces to desserts and I think we've gotten the hang of it.

For breakfast, it is good with hunks of toasted Italian bread or plain buttered scones.

Kathy's Breakfast Tofu

2 tablespoons olive oil

$1/2$ cup finely chopped onion

5 large cloves garlic, pressed or minced

$1 1/2$ pounds plum tomatoes, finely chopped (use regular tomatoes if plum type are not available)

2 tablespoons sherry or Marsala wine

2 tablespoons tamari soy sauce

4 teaspoons toasted sesame oil

1 teaspoon granulated onion or onion powder

$1/2$ teaspoon dried oregano

$1/2$ teaspoon dried basil or 2 tablespoons finely shredded fresh (use kitchen scissors or a very sharp knife)

2 pounds firm or extra-firm tofu, cut in $1/2$-inch cubes

$1/2$ teaspoon sea salt

Freshly ground black pepper

2 to 4 tablespoons plain bread crumbs (or substitute cracker crumbs from plain wheat or rye crackers)

Up to 4 tablespoons water (optional)

In a large skillet, heat oil over medium heat. Add onion and sauté for about 5 minutes, or until onion is fragrant and almost translucent. Add garlic and tomatoes, and cook, stirring often, until tomatoes release their juices and garlic is softened, about 5 minutes. Add the sherry, tamari, sesame oil, granulated onion, oregano, and dried basil, if using. Continue simmering on low heat about 5 minutes, stirring occasionally.

Add tofu and fresh basil, if using, and stir well to mix. Simmer about 5 minutes more. Add salt and pepper and adjust seasonings. Add bread crumbs—they will absorb the tomato juice and add a nice texture to the tofu. Cover and continue simmering 2 minutes. If mixture seems dry, add a little water (if using plum tomatoes, you'll probably need water, but if using regular tomatoes you probably won't) to make a thick sauce. Remove from heat and serve.

MAKES 6 TO 8 SERVINGS

While it may look like scrambled eggs, that half teaspoon of turmeric gives a surprising mild curry flavor (and just the right color). Great with whole grain toast.

Scrambled Tofu

2 teaspoons safflower oil

1 cup chopped yellow onion

1/2 cup diced celery

6 ounces (1 3/4 cups) mushrooms, thinly sliced

1 large clove garlic, minced

1 pound firm fresh tofu, rinsed and drained

2 tablespoons chopped green onions

1 tablespoon sliced pimento, roughly chopped

1 tablespoon nutritional yeast flakes

3/4 teaspoon Morga instant seasoning broth mix (powdered vegetable bouillon)

1/2 teaspoon turmeric

1/2 teaspoon Spike seasoning

1/2 teaspoon onion powder

1/2 teaspoon Vege-sal or sea salt

Freshly ground black pepper

In a medium sauté pan, heat oil over medium heat. Add onions and celery, and sauté, stirring occasionally, for 2 minutes. Add mushrooms and garlic, and sauté, stirring occasionally, until onions are tender and translucent, about 5 minutes more. Turn off heat.

Crumble tofu into vegetable mixture, keeping pieces no larger than about 3/4 inch. Add green onions, pimento, yeast, broth mix, turmeric, Spike, and onion powder. Return heat to medium and cook, stirring just until mixture is hot (5 minutes). Add Vege-sal and pepper to taste, and adjust any seasonings. Serve immediately.

MAKES 3 TO 4 SERVINGS

I have to admit I was skeptical when I first tried this, and wondered how this egg-free version would stand up. I must say it is truly delicious: distinctive, yet comfortingly familiar. A new breakfast classic. The trick here is speedy assembly with everything at the ready: Have the sauce made and held warm, steam the spinach about 20 minutes before serving, warm the wheatmeat (if using) according to package directions, poach the tofu just before assembling, and toast the muffins at the very last minute.

Tofu Benedict

1 bunch fresh spinach (about 12 ounces)

1 pound fresh, firm tofu

4 whole wheat English muffins

Butter, softened

8 thin slices wheatmeat* (optional)

2 large tomatoes, thinly sliced (need 8 slices)

1 recipe Spicy Hollandaise Sauce (page 51), kept warm in a double boiler

Paprika

8 black olives

Clean, stem, and chop spinach into large pieces. Steam until just wilted; drain well. Cover and set aside to keep warm.

Drain tofu. You will need 8 thin slices, to cover each of 8 halves of English muffin. Slice tofu accordingly (brands may vary in size and shape, and possibly contain 1 or 2 blocks per package). Poach sliced tofu by placing in a shallow pan, just covered with water; bring to a boil, then reduce heat and simmer, uncovered, 3 minutes. Drain, cover, and set aside.

*Wheatmeat is a vegetarian product made from wheat gluten. It has a chewy yet tender, meaty character. It can be purchased in the deli case fresh, like tofu, and may be called seitan, its traditional Japanese name. This is my favorite way to buy it, but you can also purchase some frozen wheatmeats in "chicken" and "beef" flavors. Use the "beef"-flavored kind in this recipe. There are also some canned products, but I find their flavor, and sometimes their ingredients, objectionable.

To assemble

Have 4 warm plates ready. Slice English muffins in half, and toast lightly in toaster or broiler. Butter lightly. If using wheatmeat, place this on the first layer, followed by the sliced tomato, several leaves of spinach, then the tofu; top with a generous ladle of Hollandaise Sauce, about $1/4$ cup per muffin half. Garnish with a light dusting of paprika and a black olive. Repeat for the other 7 halves, placing 2 muffin halves on each plate, and serve immediately.

MAKES 4 SERVINGS

While certainly not low in fat, this sauce is a delight for those vegetarians who don't eat eggs. It is a delicious and integral part of Tofu Benedict (page 49) and also makes a nice sauce for plain steamed vegetables, such as green beans or asparagus.

Because this recipe uses dairy products, we have also developed a vegan sauce using our Vegenaise, called Lemon Vegenaise Sauce (see Variation, page 52).

Spicy Hollandaise Sauce

2 cups low-fat milk

4 tablespoons ($^1/_2$ stick) unsalted butter

$^1/_2$ cup brown rice flour

1 cup sour cream

2 tablespoons freshly squeezed lemon juice

$^1/_4$ teaspoon onion powder

$^1/_4$ teaspoon sea salt

$^1/_8$ teaspoon turmeric

Dash of cayenne

Dash of freshly ground white pepper

Scald milk in a small saucepan and set aside. (To scald milk: Heat over medium heat in saucepan until milk is hot and small bubbles form around rim of pan; milk will not be simmering or boiling yet.) In a medium saucepan, melt butter over low heat. Gradually whisk in flour and continue whisking until smooth. Stir almost constantly for about 1 minute, or until flour has a fragrant roasted smell. Slowly whisk in hot milk, whisking constantly to avoid lumps. Stir in the sour cream, lemon juice, onion powder, salt, turmeric, cayenne, and pepper. Increase heat to medium, and stir constantly until sauce is thickened and just below the boil, about 5 minutes. Serve immediately or keep warm over low heat in a double boiler.

The sauce can be prepared up to 2 days ahead. Refrigerate when cooled, and reheat in a double boiler. You may need to add more milk to correct consistency when reheating.

variation Lemon Vegenaise Sauce Stir together: $^1/_2$ cup Vegenaise, 1 to 2 tablespoons freshly squeezed lemon juice, a dash of turmeric, and a dash of cayenne pepper. Serve immediately, or refrigerate until needed. This can be served cold or brought to room temperature, or it can be warmed carefully as we do at the restaurant. Heat it in the top of a double boiler over simmering water, or over low heat in a small saucepan, whisking just until warm. Overheating will cause the sauce to break.

MAKES 3 CUPS

Salads, Dressings, and Sides

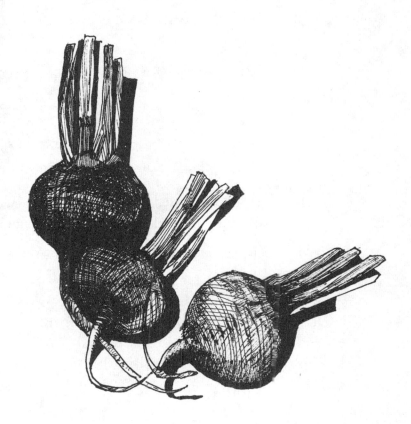

This is a crisp and flavorful vegetarian version of Chinese chicken salad. In the heat of summer, when cooking energy is scarce, this is the perfect main-dish salad. You can omit the rice noodles if you're cutting back on fried foods or carbohydrates—the salad will still be delicious.

Chinese Tofu Salad

1/2 cup (2 ounces) slivered almonds

1 large head romaine or 2 romaine hearts

1 ounce rice stick noodles* (optional) or 3 cups shredded Chinese cabbage

Peanut or safflower oil for frying

10 to 12 ounces seasoned tofu, cut into thin 2-inch-long matchsticks

DRESSING

1/2 cup seasoned rice vinegar**

4 teaspoons honey

1 tablespoon minced pickled ginger

1 teaspoon pickled ginger juice (optional, saved from the pickled ginger)

2 to 4 teaspoons toasted (also called Oriental) sesame oil

Preheat oven to 300°F. Toast slivered almonds on a baking sheet in the oven for 10 to 12 minutes, or until just golden and fragrant. Set aside to cool.

Slice romaine into thin (3/8-inch) shreds. Wash, spin dry, and place in serving bowl.

Fry rice noodles if using. To fry the noodles, heat 2 inches oil in a wok or deep, heavy skillet to about 375°F (use a deep-fry thermometer or test a small piece of noodle in the oil. It should sizzle and puff up immediately, but not burn). Separate the noodles into small batches, otherwise they won't cook through. Toss

*Rice sticks are a dried rice noodle. You can find them at Asian groceries, natural food stores, and many supermarkets.
**Seasoned rice vinegar is made from rice, to which salt and sugar have been added. It's the traditional seasoning for the rice in sushi and nori rolls. Most supermarkets carry it—Marukan is my favorite supermarket brand. Spectrum makes a natural foods version, which is sweetened with juice concentrate instead of sugar, available at natural food stores.

in the first handful, all at once, which should puff up immediately. Drain with a slotted spoon and place on paper towels. Continue as above until all noodles are fried. If using cabbage, add to shredded lettuce and toss; if using noodles, set aside.

Whisk together vinegar, honey, pickled ginger, ginger juice (if using), and sesame oil. Just before serving, toss the lettuce mixture with the noodles and enough dressing to coat lettuce lightly (you may not need all of it). Lay strips of tofu across top of salad and garnish with the toasted almonds. Serve immediately.

MAKES 2 MAIN-DISH OR 4 SMALL SERVINGS

Tofu replaces chicken in this colorful crunchy salad, adapted from a James Beard recipe.

Wild rice is in fact not a true rice, but the seed of an aquatic Native American plant. It's a bit of a trick to cook, though it is more forgiving than brown rice. You may need more water than called for, and the time can vary: It often takes 30 to 60 minutes from start to finish, depending on the length of the grains, their freshness, and quality. The best wild rice is still harvested by Native Americans and is truly a wild plant. Hybrid "wild rice" is farmed, and is not as flavorful, but is somewhat less expensive. Either kind · can be used in this recipe.

Wild Rice and Tofu Salad

1/2 cup wild rice

1 1/2 cups water

1/4 teaspoon sea salt

10 ounces firm tofu

2 tablespoons Westbrae Tofu Sauce* or tamari soy or teriyaki sauce

1 cup chopped watercress

1/2 cup diced celery

1/4 cup finely chopped green onions

1/2 cup (2 ounces) blanched almonds, toasted** and chopped

TARRAGON VINAIGRETTE

1/3 cup extra-virgin olive oil

3 tablespoons white wine vinegar or tarragon-flavored white vinegar

2 1/2 tablespoons chopped fresh tarragon or 3/4 teaspoon dried

Dash of cayenne pepper

 Rinse rice under running water. In a medium saucepan, bring rice, water, and salt to a rapid boil, then reduce heat to simmer. Cover and cook until

*Westbrae Tofu Sauce is a seasoned soy-based sauce with Asian flavorings, available at natural food stores.
**To toast almonds, place whole blanched almonds on a cookie sheet, and toast in a preheated 300°F oven for 10 to 15 minutes, or until light golden and fragrant. Remove immediately from pan and allow to cool before chopping.

grains puff open and white interior of rice can be seen. Check it after 30 minutes. If the water's gone but the rice isn't tender and fluffy, then add 1/2 to 1 cup water; bring again to a boil, then reduce heat and continue simmering, covered, checking every 10 minutes. Lifting the lid won't harm it, and if at the end the rice is tender but there's still water in the pan, you can just drain it in a sieve. It won't become sticky like regular rice. And it doesn't have to be completely fluffy to be done; a few al dente kernels will be just fine.

Transfer rice to a large bowl and allow to cool to room temperature.

While rice is cooking, steam tofu for 10 minutes. (This process makes tofu firmer and will help it to absorb the marinade.) Immediately place the hot tofu in a bowl, and pour the tofu sauce over it. Toss gently to cover. Let the tofu marinate for at least 1/2 hour, then add it to the cooled rice along with the marinade, watercress, celery, and onions. Chill mixture briefly before serving, or up to several hours.

To make the vinaigrette: In a medium bowl, slowly whisk oil into vinegar. Stir in tarragon and cayenne. Pour a small amount of vinaigrette over chilled salad and toss gently, adding more vinaigrette a little at a time until salad is evenly coated (you may not need all the dressing). Garnish with toasted almonds; serve immediately.

MAKES 4 SERVINGS

Use the freshest spinach available. Gorgeous color makes this salad very appealing, and the vinaigrette contributes robust flavor, yet is deceptively simple.

Warm spinach salad

1 bunch (about 12 ounces) fresh spinach

6 medium mushrooms, sliced

1 large tomato, cut in 8 wedges

1 small red onion, cut in thin rings

Homemade Croutons (page 59)

BALSAMIC VINAIGRETTE

1/2 cup extra-virgin olive oil

1/4 cup balsamic vinegar

1 small clove garlic, minced or pressed

Sea salt

Freshly ground black pepper

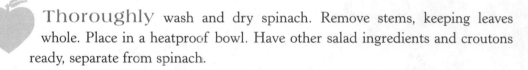

Thoroughly wash and dry spinach. Remove stems, keeping leaves whole. Place in a heatproof bowl. Have other salad ingredients and croutons ready, separate from spinach.

In a small bowl, whisk together oil, vinegar, garlic, and salt and pepper to taste. Simmer in a small saucepan, uncovered, until just beginning to bubble. Remove from heat.

Pour hot dressing over spinach, and toss to wilt slightly. Add mushrooms, tomato, onion, and croutons and lightly toss. Serve immediately.

MAKES 2 LARGE OR 4 SMALL SALADS

There is nothing like fresh, crunchy, homemade croutons. To make them, let your bread become nice and stale (a few days in a paper bag will do, but not so hard you can't slice it). Experiment with designer breads for exciting flavors and textures, such as bread flavored with pesto, rosemary, olives, or walnuts; you can vary the added herbs as well.

Croutons

2 to 3 tablespoons olive oil

1 1/2 cups cubed (1/2 inch) stale whole wheat or French bread

1 clove garlic, minced or pressed

1/4 teaspoon dried thyme

Sea salt

In a large skillet, place oil over medium-low heat. When oil is hot, add bread, garlic, thyme, and salt to taste. Stir often, tossing the cubes to brown them evenly, until they are nicely browned all over and fragrant, 7 to 10 minutes. Remove from heat and place on paper towels to absorb excess oil. When cool, store in airtight container for up to 1 week. Use in Warm Spinach Salad (page 58) or another green salad.

As an alternative, you may bake the croutons. In that case, preheat your oven to 375°F. Toss the cubed bread with the other ingredients. Place on 1 or 2 large baking sheets, and bake until croutons are crispy and golden, 10 to 15 minutes. Cool and store as above.

MAKES 1 1/2 CUPS

There are so many versions of this salad. Surprisingly, you can make a great rendition without the eggs or the anchovies. Vegenaise produces the needed creaminess, and vegetarian Worcestershire sauce provides piquant notes.

For extra protein, add seasoned, marinated tofu.

Easier Caesar

DRESSING

1/4 cup freshly squeezed lemon juice

1 tablespoon vegetarian Worcestershire-style* sauce

1 tablespoon Vegenaise or eggless mayonnaise

2 small cloves garlic

3/4 cup olive oil

Sea salt

CROUTONS

1 small stale baguette or loaf of country French bread (with a fairly tender crust), cut into 3/4-inch cubes to equal 4 cups

1/4 cup olive oil

3 cloves garlic, minced

2 teaspoons finely chopped fresh rosemary

3 to 4 heads romaine lettuce hearts, torn (about 12 cups; look for organic romaine hearts, prewashed, at your market)

1/2 cup freshly grated imported Parmesan cheese

8 to 10 ounces seasoned tofu or half of a recipe of Marinated Tofu (page 139), cut into strips or cubes (optional)

To prepare dressing: In a blender container, place lemon juice, Worcestershire, Vegenaise, and garlic. Blend until smooth. With blender running, slowly pour in oil (mixture will be creamy). Add salt to taste; set aside.

*Traditional Worcestershire sauce contains anchovies. If you wish to avoid this, there are vegetarian versions of this sauce available at natural food stores.

To prepare croutons: Preheat oven to 350°F. Toss together cubed bread, oil, garlic, and rosemary, coating bread evenly. Place on 2 large baking sheets and bake for about 20 minutes, or until croutons are golden and toasty. Remove from oven and allow to cool. (After cooling, if not using right away, store in airtight containers.)

To prepare salad: Toss romaine with dressing, Parmesan, and croutons. (You'll probably need only half of the prepared dressing; store the rest in refrigerator. It will keep for a couple of weeks.) Place tofu strips on top, if using. Serve immediately.

Variation To make the easiest of Caesars, you could skip our dressing recipe altogether, and go straight to Follow Your Heart and buy one of our bottled Caesar dressings, in both dairy and vegan versions.

MAKES 6 REGULAR SALAD (NOT MAIN-DISH) SERVINGS

A proper tabbouleh is mostly salad, with just enough bulghur wheat to hold it together. This one is full of fresh vegetables and is made with quinoa (pronounced keen-wah), a tiny, ancient grain from South America, which makes an excellent substitute for bulghur wheat. Quinoa cooks up fast and fluffy, is high in calcium, and has more protein than any other grain. My good friend Kim Schiffer is known as the "Queen of Quinoa," because she invented this and many other recipes featuring this versatile grain.

Make sure your parsley and mint are dark green and very fresh.

Quinoa Tabbouleh

1 cup quinoa, rinsed in a fine sieve and drained well

1 3/4 cups water

2 medium carrots, finely diced

4 plum tomatoes, chopped

1 large cucumber, diced

1 cup chopped fresh mint

1 cup finely chopped fresh parsley

1/2 cup finely chopped red onion

2 cloves garlic, minced (optional)

2/3 cup olive oil

1/2 cup freshly squeezed lemon juice

1 teaspoon freshly ground black pepper

1/2 teaspoon sea salt

1 cup Greek black olives (optional)

In a 2-quart saucepan, bring quinoa and water to a boil. Skim off any bubbles that foam up (this is naturally occurring saponin in the quinoa that can have a bitter taste if it remains), then reduce heat and simmer, covered, for about 15 minutes, until all water is absorbed. Remove from heat, uncover, and allow to cool.

Place the cooled quinoa in a large bowl. Add the carrots, tomatoes, cucumber, mint, parsley, onion, and garlic, if using. In a separate bowl, whisk together the oil, lemon juice, pepper, and salt. Pour over quinoa mixture, using only as much as necessary to coat well. Toss thoroughly. Garnish with olives and serve.

MAKES 4 TO 6 SERVINGS

My friend Ray brought this over for dinner one night, inspired by impeccably fresh string beans and radicchio he'd bought at the farmer's market, and voilà—a salad was born. Try to buy two kinds of beans for a visual treat, such as haricots vert (the tender young French green beans) mixed with yellow wax beans.

Ray's Beans

1 pound fresh string beans, preferably $^1/_2$ pound each haricots vert and yellow wax beans

3 to 4 tablespoons extra-virgin olive oil

1 leek, well washed and finely chopped, both white and green parts (for leek-washing directions see page 91)

$^1/_2$ red onion, finely chopped (about $^1/_3$ cup)

$^1/_2$ cup torn radicchio leaves (2-inch pieces)

1 tablespoon red wine vinegar or your choice of an herb-infused vinegar, matching the herb used below, such as tarragon- or basil-flavored white wine vinegar, or use raspberry-infused white wine vinegar

Several leaves fresh tarragon or basil, finely chopped

Sea salt

Freshly ground black pepper

Remove stem ends from beans. In a pot fitted with a steamer, steam beans 8 to 10 minutes, or until they are barely tender and color is still bright. (If you use different types of beans, they may require different cooking times if one type is much larger than another, in which case steam them separately. It's important not to overcook beans.) Immediately rinse with cold water to stop further cooking, and set aside.

In a large skillet, heat 3 tablespoons oil over medium heat. Add leek and onion, and sauté, stirring occasionally, until leek and onion are both tender and sweet, about 10 minutes. Add radicchio and heat for 1 minute, just until slightly wilted. Remove from heat, and toss with drained beans. Season with vinegar, tarragon, salt, and pepper to taste. Add the last tablespoon of oil now if you think it needs it. Serve at room temperature.

MAKES 4 SERVINGS

This hearty salad makes a great main dish for lunch. There is something wonderful about the crispy warm potatoes, the mustardy dressing, and the spicy greens.

Serve the salad at room temperature. Once the greens are added, you must serve it right away, because the greens will begin to wilt. Like Cinderella, there is a limited window of opportunity.

By the way, the roasted potatoes are fabulous on their own, without the greens, vinegar, or mustard; use them to accompany a main dish or soup.

Roasted Potato and Watercress Salad

$^1/_4$ cup olive oil

1 tablespoon minced garlic

1 teaspoon sea salt

1 teaspoon finely chopped fresh rosemary or $^1/_4$ teaspoon dried

$^1/_2$ teaspoon freshly ground black pepper

$^1/_2$ teaspoon dried thyme

2$^1/_2$ pounds small to medium red potatoes, scrubbed, skins left on, then sliced into thin wedges, lengthwise (about 8 wedges per potato, or cut as necessary to make large bite-sized pieces)

2 tablespoons white wine vinegar or an herbal vinegar such as basil- or tarragon-flavored white wine vinegar

2 teaspoons Dijon mustard

$^1/_4$ cup chopped green onions

1 bunch watercress, stemmed (or a small bunch arugula), torn into bite-sized pieces

Preheat oven to 400°F. In a large bowl, whisk together the oil, garlic, salt, rosemary, pepper, and thyme. Add the potato wedges and stir to coat them evenly with oil mixture. Arrange potatoes on a baking sheet so that pieces don't touch each other, and roast until potatoes are nicely browned and tender, about 40 minutes.

Meanwhile, whisk together the vinegar and mustard in a large bowl. When potatoes are finished baking, toss them, while still very warm, with the vinegar mixture; they will absorb the flavors better this way. Let potatoes cool a bit, so they are not too warm to wilt the greens. Then add the onions and watercress. Toss to coat greens thoroughly. Serve right away.

MAKES 4 TO 6 SERVINGS

This is perfect for potlucks, where it quickly disappears. It's one of those dishes that looks as good as it tastes: thin, square-cut udon noodles are tossed with ginger, cilantro, sesame oil, and chiles. Crisp sugar snap peas, slivered zucchini, and circles of carrots are sprinkled throughout. Kids love it too, although I usually cut back on the crushed chiles for them.

szechuan Noodle salad

One 8-ounce package udon noodles, preferably all wheat (available at natural food stores and Asian groceries)

$1/3$ cup Vegenaise or mayonnaise

2 tablespoons tamari soy sauce

$1^1/2$ tablespoons hot pepper sesame oil*

1 tablespoon freshly grated peeled ginger (A Chinese bamboo ginger grater makes quick work of this or use the fine blade of a grater or process in a food processor.)

2 teaspoons brown rice vinegar

2 large cloves garlic, minced ($1^1/2$ teaspoons)

$1/2$ teaspoon crushed red chiles

1 carrot, cut thinly on the diagonal

1 medium zucchini, cut into thin sticks about 2 inches long

4 ounces fresh sugar snap or snow peas, stemmed, halved if large

$1/4$ cup chopped green onions

$1/4$ cup chopped fresh cilantro

1 tablespoon raw sesame seeds

7 or 8 ounces seasoned spicy or teriyaki tofu (optional)

Bring 3 quarts unsalted water to a boil. Add noodles and cook, uncovered, over medium heat, until noodles are al dente, 7 or 8 minutes. Immediately drain, then rinse noodles in cold water; drain again thoroughly. Cover and set aside.

*If you can't find hot pepper sesame oil, which is a mix of peppers and toasted sesame oil, use regular toasted sesame oil and add more crushed red chiles.

MIX together the Vegenaise, tamari, sesame oil, ginger, vinegar garlic, and chiles and set aside. Steam the carrot, zucchini, and snow peas separately, for a few minutes each, just until each vegetable is tender but still brightly colored. Cool, then toss with the sauce, noodles, onions, cilantro, and sesame seeds. If using tofu, slice into thin strips and toss gently into salad. Serve cold or at room temperature. (This keeps well, refrigerated, for a couple of days.)

MAKES 4 SERVINGS

This simple dressing is delicious on a variety of green salads. Using the same proportions, you can change the types of oils, vinegars, and seasonings to create your own vinaigrette. Walnut oil has a mild nutty flavor—dinner guests always notice it, favorably. Make sure it is very fresh.

simple vinaigrette

$1/2$ cup walnut oil (pale colored, purchased at natural food stores—this is not the intensely flavored roasted French oil purchased at specialty shops)

$1/4$ cup extra-virgin olive oil

3 tablespoons red wine vinegar

$1/2$ teaspoon Dijon mustard (optional)

Sea salt

Freshly ground white or black pepper

Place all ingredients plus salt and pepper to taste in a pint mason jar, screw lid on tightly, and shake vigorously until well mixed. Be sure to shake again right before dressing salad.

MAKES ABOUT 1 CUP

It is no secret: I love beets, with their earthy flavor and glorious magenta color. Unless, of course, you are using golden beets, which really do have golden flesh, or those Italian Chioggia beets, which are deep pink with white stripes.

Peeling raw beets is a nasty job. To avoid this, I steam them, unpeeled; after cooling, the skins slip right off. You can also bake the beets, which results in a slightly deeper flavor. To bake beets, place small beets in a roasting pan with a few tablespoons of water. Cover tightly and bake at 375°F for 35 to 40 minutes, or until beets are tender. Again, peel when cooled.

Devour this salad in spring, when beets are at their sweet best. And don't forget the beet greens. Save them for another use: I love to steam or sauté them just until tender, and season with a little butter and balsamic vinegar. They have a velvety texture and taste like mild chard.

Beet and Red Onion Salad

2 pounds small red beets, weighed without greens (if small beets are unavailable, about 2 bunches large beets)

3 small red onions, peeled, quartered, and thinly sliced

$1/3$ cup extra-virgin olive oil

2 tablespoons red wine vinegar

2 teaspoons balsamic vinegar

Sea salt

Freshly ground black pepper

Wash and trim ends of beets. Leaving them unpeeled, steam the whole beets until just tender, approximately 30 minutes, depending on size of beets. Let cool; peels will slide off easily. Cut into large cubes about 1 inch square, or simply halve or quarter them if they are small.

Meanwhile, soak sliced onions in 2 cups cold water for about 40 minutes (this takes the bite out of the onions, but they will still be quite flavorful).

With a whisk, blend oil into vinegars. Toss together beets, onions, and dressing. Add salt and pepper to taste. Serve cold or at room temperature.

MAKES 6 SERVINGS

It's funny what we call Italian dressing in America. In Italy, salad dressing is likely to be just great olive oil, some aged wine vinegar, and a pinch of salt, often mixed right at the table.

Which is not to say this isn't delicious. Herbs and spices added to this dressing make it "Italian" in America. Use very fresh oils and a vinegar you love. Vinegars vary greatly, just as wines and olive oils do; many are too acidic for me. Make sure your dried herbs are fresh—six months to a year is the maximum shelf life of dried green herbs, and that's if they're stored in a cool place. If they're next to the stove or exposed to light, they won't last as long.

Taste your ingredients first. The better their quality, the better your dressing will be, and everything else you cook.

Italian Dressing

1/2 cup extra-virgin olive oil

1/2 cup safflower oil

1/3 cup water

1/4 cup basil- or tarragon-flavored white wine vinegar

2 1/2 tablespoons freshly squeezed lemon juice

1 small clove garlic, pressed or minced

2 teaspoons mild honey

1 teaspoon dried basil

1 teaspoon dried parsley

1/2 teaspoon sea salt

1/2 teaspoon dried oregano

1/4 teaspoon freshly ground black pepper

1/4 teaspoon white pepper

1/4 teaspoon dried thyme

 Combine all ingredients in blender container and blend until smooth, about 10 seconds. Store in refrigerator.

MAKES 1 1/4 CUPS

I have always loved the flavor of ranch dressing. As a kid, I loved to buy those little seasoning packets, add buttermilk or mayo, and shake. Unfortunately, many commercial dressings, especially the packets, contain MSG and other nasty stuff, like preservatives and artificial flavorings.

This dressing makes kids want to eat salad.

Ranch-Style Dressing

$1/2$ cup buttermilk or plain yogurt

1 green onion, coarsely chopped

1 tablespoon white wine vinegar

1 tablespoon minced fresh parsley

1 tablespoon minced fresh basil

1 small clove garlic, minced (optional)

$1/2$ teaspoon dried basil

$3/4$ cup Vegenaise or mayonnaise

Sea salt

Freshly ground black pepper

Combine the buttermilk, onion, vinegar, parsley, fresh basil, garlic (if using), and dried basil in a blender container. Blend a few seconds, just until smooth. Pour into another container; gently whisk in the Vegenaise, and the salt and pepper to taste. Serve on a crisp green salad, or as a dip for raw or steamed veggies.

MAKES 1 1/4 CUPS

I loved the idea of poppy seeds before I ever tasted them, because poppy seed cakes were featured in one of my favorite childhood fairy tales. While I do not have a recipe for those mythical cakes, I offer you this—a recipe from our friend Amy Lenzo of San Diego. The poppy seeds add texture and color as well as their distinct flavor to this pretty dressing. Tart and sweet, it is great on a mixed green salad and makes an excellent dressing for sliced, red, ripe tomatoes.

Tarragon-Poppy Seed Dressing

1/4 cup brown rice vinegar

3 tablespoons water

2 tablespoons mild honey

2 tablespoons Dijon mustard

1 1/2 teaspoons small capers

1/2 teaspoon dried tarragon

1/2 teaspoon dried parsley

1/2 teaspoon fresh minced garlic

1/4 teaspoon sea salt

1/4 teaspoon freshly ground black pepper

1 1/2 cups Vegenaise or mayonnaise

1/2 teaspoon poppy seeds

In a blender container, combine the vinegar, water, honey, mustard, capers, tarragon, parsley, garlic, salt, and pepper. Blend until smooth, 20 to 30 seconds. Add Vegenaise and blend another 3 to 5 seconds, just until mixed thoroughly. Stir in poppy seeds and serve. (Poppy seeds should not be blended.)

MAKES ABOUT 1 1/2 CUPS

Home-cooked beans are a basic staple of the home table. It's so easy to open a can of beans, but they taste much better when freshly cooked, and they aren't difficult to make. You've just got to remember to soak them the night before, or try the emergency boil method below. So if you've got the time... make them from scratch.

You can cook most kinds of beans pretty much the same way, except the cooking times will vary. Pinto beans are faster. Black beans tend to be harder, so they take longer.

Use these beans to make Bob's Breakfast (page 42) or use them in our Black Bean Tostadas or Burritos (page 110).

Basic Black Beans

2 cups dried black beans (the small variety, not the large black soybeans)

1 teaspoon sea salt

Wash beans well and remove any rocks or broken pieces. Place in a large bowl and cover with several inches of fresh water; let sit overnight or for 8 hours at cool room temperature. Drain, discarding soaking water. (Quick-soak method: Bring washed beans and 4 cups water to a boil; reduce heat and simmer, covered, 5 minutes. Turn off heat; let beans sit for 1 hour, covered, in the hot water. Proceed.)

If using overnight soaked beans, place drained beans in the pot with 4 cups water. If using quick-soak method, place 2 cups fresh water in pot with beans and their soaking water. In either case, bring beans and water to a boil, reduce heat to medium-low, and cook, partially covered, for 1 to $1^{1}/_{2}$ hours, adding more water if necessary. It's important to keep beans covered with water at all times, until they are almost tender; toward the end of the cooking time, beans will become tender and broth will be smooth and thick. Add salt and remove from heat.

MAKES ABOUT 4 CUPS

Do you want to know a perfectly satisfying vegetarian dinner that is easy to make? Bake some potatoes. Make this Mushroom-Garlic Sauce. Make a simple pot of Cream of Broccoli Soup (page 99). Make our Easier Caesar salad with tofu (page 60) and hold the croutons. Serve it up. It'll take you an hour or less, and with careful planning you'll have some great leftovers (bake extra potatoes for Breakfast Potatoes, page 44; make extra soup and salad for lunch).

This is also a wonderful sauce for our Stuffed Potatoes (page 138), plain mashed potatoes, or as gravy for Kasha Potato Pie (page 116).

Mushroom-Garlic Sauce

8 ounces whole small mushrooms, washed and trimmed

1 tablespoon safflower oil

1 tablespoon tamari soy sauce

1 medium clove garlic, minced

$1/2$ teaspoon dried basil

Place all ingredients in a 9-inch shallow saucepan and cook over low heat, stirring occasionally, just until mushrooms are tender, about 10 minutes. Mixture should be quite juicy with mushroom liquid. Add more basil if desired.

The sauce may be cooled and refrigerated; reheat briefly before serving.

MAKES ABOUT 4 SERVINGS

People will not believe how simple this is. The smell of roasting garlic will permeate your house, and it reminds me of a Chinese restaurant.

Cabbage with Garlic

2 tablespoons olive oil

3 to 4 whole cloves garlic

1 medium green or red cabbage, quartered, then sliced very thinly

1 tablespoon tamari soy sauce

In a skillet large enough to hold all the cabbage, heat the oil over medium heat until it is hot but not smoking. Add the garlic, and sauté, turning over occasionally, until it is golden brown all over. Add the cabbage, and keep it moving—turn it over occasionally, and continue sautéing for 5 minutes.

Add the tamari and keep stirring. If it seems dry, add a couple tablespoons of water, but it shouldn't get very liquid—just enough to keep it from sticking. Cover and continue cooking for about 5 minutes, or until cabbage is tender. Serve immediately.

MAKES 4 TO 6 SERVINGS

You can make this as spicy as you like, depending on the peppers you use. This refreshing chutney is brilliant green. Use it to accent Indian foods, such as Mrs. Singh's Red Lentils (page 121). This recipe comes from Indian cooking teacher and author Neelam Batra.

Cilantro and Mint Chutney

2 bunches cilantro, stemmed

1 bunch mint, stemmed

1 bunch green onions, chopped

2 serrano peppers or 2 tablespoons diced green bell pepper

Juice of 2 medium limes

$1/2$ teaspoon ground coriander

$1/2$ teaspoon ground cumin

Sea salt

 In a food processor, briefly blend cilantro, mint, onions, peppers, and lime juice. Add coriander, cumin, and salt to taste and blend again until smooth.

Serve with appetizers or with dinner. Holds well in refrigerator for about 2 months; can also be frozen.

MAKES 1 $1/2$ TO 2 CUPS

Chile, ginger, and garam masala turn these ordinary vegetables into a feast fit for a raj.

Indian spinach with carrots and scallions

2 pounds spinach, stemmed and washed thoroughly

2 tablespoons safflower oil or ghee (Indian-style clarified butter)

2 large carrots, cut into thin diagonals

6 green onions, minced

2 teaspoons grated peeled fresh ginger

$1/2$ to 1 teaspoon minced hot green chile (such as serrano pepper)

Sea salt

Pinch of raw sugar

$1/2$ teaspoon Garam Masala (page 122)

Place spinach in a large pot with the water still clinging to the leaves. Turn heat to high and cook, covered, until spinach is wilted, about 5 minutes. (Check it occasionally.) Drain and set aside. When cool, chop spinach finely.

Heat oil in a wide, heavy skillet over medium heat. Put in the carrots and sauté a few minutes, or until carrots start to become tender. Add the onions, ginger, and chile, and cook a few more minutes, until onions are wilted and carrots are just tender. Add spinach, salt to taste, and sugar, and stir to heat through. Remove from heat and add Garam Masala; mix well. Serve at once.

MAKES 6 TO 8 SERVINGS

The spinach cooks down into concentrated morsels, deep green and elegant, with contrasting dark color from the slightly bitter, purple radicchio. A great side dish with pasta.

Sautéed Spinach and Radicchio

2 tablespoons olive oil

6 to 8 ounces radicchio, cut in 1- to 2-inch pieces

1 1/2 pounds spinach, washed thoroughly and stemmed

Balsamic vinegar

Tamari soy sauce

In a very large skillet or sauté pan, heat oil over medium heat. Add radicchio and sauté, stirring frequently, for about 5 minutes, or until radicchio darkens and is slightly tender. Add half of the spinach; cook, stirring, until spinach begins to wilt. Add rest of spinach and continue cooking and stirring 3 or 4 minutes, or until all the spinach is wilted and tender, but still bright green. Turn off heat. Season with a few teaspoons balsamic vinegar and tamari to taste. Serve immediately.

MAKES 4 SERVINGS

This is a fluffy jewel of a rice dish. Red salsa adds color and a dash of spiciness, and it's lower in fat than traditional versions. Perfect with Mexican entrees such as Enchiladas Verde (page 112).

spanish Rice

1 tablespoon olive oil

1/4 cup finely chopped yellow onion

1 large clove garlic, minced

1 cup white basmati rice

1 1/2 cups water

3/4 cup mild tomato salsa

3/4 teaspoon ground cumin

3/4 teaspoon sea salt

1/2 teaspoon chili powder

In a heavy-bottomed, 3-quart saucepan, heat oil over medium heat. Add onion and sauté, stirring occasionally, for about 3 minutes, until onion is fragrant and a little golden. Add garlic and rice and continue cooking, stirring occasionally, until rice is slightly roasted and fragrant and onion is translucent, about 5 minutes. Add water, salsa, cumin, salt, and chili powder and bring to a boil. Reduce heat to lowest simmer and cook, covered, 15 to 20 minutes, or until all water is absorbed and rice is tender and fluffy. Serve warm.

MAKES 4 SERVINGS

Indians use spices so freely and so well. They even have special tins to hold the spices. I have one at home: a large round stainless-steel tin, with a tight-fitting lid. Inside, small cups are nestled to hold about ten different spices. So when you're cooking, you just open the tin, and grab a pinch of this and a pinch of that. If you ever go to buy these spices at an Indian grocery, it is nothing like the spice aisle in an American market. There are big bags of cumin seed and big bags of cinnamon sticks. It is much more economical to buy them this way, and if you cook Indian food often, you'll go through spices like you won't believe! These tantalizing spices infuse basmati rice with wonderful flavor, and basmati rice is already flavorful on its own—even dry, it has a distinctive, sweet perfume, rather like jasmine. Are you hungry yet?

Before you run off and start cooking, let me tell you a bit more. Black cardamom has a smoky flavor, and is hard to find outside an Indian grocery; but the regular green cardamom will do. Just make sure to use whole pods, not just the seeds. And serve this recipe sometime with Paneer (page 82). It's easy to make and adds another dimension to the Spiced Rice.

Spiced Rice

1 tablespoon safflower oil or ghee (Indian-style clarified butter)

1 small onion, finely chopped

3/4 teaspoon whole cumin seeds

1 1/2 cups white basmati rice, washed and drained well

4 whole black cardamom pods, available at Asian groceries (if unavailable, use green or white cardamom)

One 1-inch stick cinnamon

1/2 teaspoon ground coriander

1/2 teaspoon sea salt

3 cups water

1 cup fresh or frozen green peas (if fresh, steam briefly until tender; if frozen, rinse with hot water to thaw; optional)

¹/₂ recipe Paneer (page 82), drained and pressed, or 6 to 8 ounces firm tofu, fried* (optional)

In a 10-inch deep sauté pan, heat the oil and sauté onion over medium heat until golden, 5 to 7 minutes. Stir in cumin and cook for about 2 minutes, stirring often; add rice, cardamom, cinnamon, coriander, and salt. Stir to coat rice with oil and cook 1 minute.

Add water and bring to a boil; reduce heat to simmer, and cook, covered, about 20 minutes, or until all water is absorbed. If using peas, add them to the warm cooked rice, stirring gently to fluff rice and mix in. If using Paneer or tofu, gently place on top of rice; serve

MAKES 4 SERVINGS

*If you'd like to add protein to this dish, as well as rich flavor and interesting texture add some cubes of paneer (a fresh Indian cheese) or tofu. Cut into ¹/₂-inch-by-³/₄-inch cubes. Place 1 or 2 tablespoons vegetable oil or ghee in a heavy sauté pan over medium heat. When oil is hot but not smoking, add paneer or tofu. Fry gently, turning pieces often, adjusting heat as necessary, for 4 to 6 minutes, or until paneer or tofu is lightly golden. Drain on paper towels and serve warm on top of rice.

Paneer is a sweet, fresh Indian cheese that you can make easily at home. When you add yogurt to heated milk, it separates into curds and whey, as in Little Miss Muffet's nursery rhyme. The whey is a nutritious sweet drink, which you could add to homemade bread or soup, or even to your garden—it seems a shame to throw it out.

The curds are drained and pressed, turning it into this simple cheese. The cheese can be fried or added to other dishes. We use it in our recipe for Spiced Rice (page 80). It is often paired with peas (matar paneer) or spinach (saag paneer), which we don't include here, but they are easy to find in most Indian cookbooks.

This is another recipe from my friend, cooking teacher and cookbook author Neelam Batra, who makes Indian cooking simple.

Paneer

8 cups low-fat milk*

2 cups plain full-fat yogurt*

Bring milk to a boil and stir in yogurt. When milk curdles and water looks semi-transparent, remove from heat. Drain through a double layer of cheese-cloth (I use a sheer piece of nylon fabric that can be washed and reused). Tie the cheesecloth into a bag to surround the cheese, and hang it from your faucet—its own weight will remove the water and it can drain into the sink. Let it hang there for about 1/2 hour. You can then use the cheese as is, or you can further shape it by pressing the cheese under a heavy weight (a large pan of water is heavy enough), further removing moisture, and shaping the cheese into a rectangle that is easy to cut. Press for another 1/2 hour. Remove weight and cloth, and cut cheese into desired shapes or sizes, or crumble it, as the recipe requires.

MAKES 12 OUNCES TO 1 POUND PANEER

*You can switch these around—use full-fat milk and low-fat yogurt—but make sure one of them has all the fat, or you'll get less volume and the cheese won't taste very creamy. I don't recommend using nonfat products in this for the same reason. It is ok to use full-fat milk and full-fat yogurt, however; that will give the most volume and the best flavor and texture.

The flavor of fried rice is captured here with a lot less oil. It's very pretty, with its green onion, tiny diced carrots, and red and yellow bell peppers.

Good with Stir-Fried Broccoli with Mushrooms, Red Onion, and Seasoned Tofu (page 136).

Confetti Rice

1 tablespoon safflower or sesame oil

$1/2$ cup chopped green onions

$1/2$ cup diced carrots

$1/4$ cup diced red bell pepper

$1/4$ cup diced yellow bell pepper

2 cloves garlic, minced

1 cup long-grain white rice

$1/2$ teaspoon sea salt

2 cups water

$1/2$ cup peas, fresh or frozen (thawed), cooked just until tender and bright green

In a 9-inch sauté pan, heat the oil over medium heat. Add the onions, carrots, peppers, and garlic, and sauté, stirring often, for about 5 minutes, or until vegetables are a little tender and garlic is lightly golden. Add rice and continue cooking for 2 minutes. Stir well to coat rice with oil. Add salt and water; bring to a boil. Reduce heat to low and simmer, covered, about 15 minutes, or until all water is absorbed. Remove from heat, and gently stir in peas. Serve.

MAKES 4 SERVINGS

Sandwiches and Soups

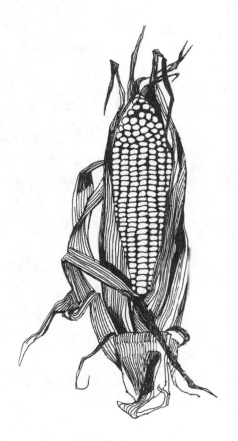

Say farewell to chicken with this yummy salad. Tempeh is gently roasted, creating a nutty flavor and a slightly crisp texture; then, while still warm, it is mixed with the remaining ingredients to better combine flavors.

Bye-Bye Birdie (Tempeh Salad)

1 tablespoon olive oil

12 ounces plain tempeh (use Surata Soyfoods brand if available)

1 cup chopped celery (about 3 large stalks)

3/4 cup Vegenaise or eggless mayonnaise

1/4 cup chopped green onions

Sea salt (optional)

Preheat oven to 350°F. Brush oil on a large baking sheet and crumble the tempeh into approximately 1/2-inch pieces; distribute on baking sheet evenly. Bake for 10 minutes, or until edges of tempeh are just slightly dry; they should not be brown or very crisp. Let cool about 5 minutes.

Meanwhile, place celery, Vegenaise, and onions in large bowl. Add warm tempeh and stir. Mash all ingredients slightly with a potato masher to blend. Taste and add salt if desired, although you may not need it. Chill and serve as a salad or sandwich filling.

MAKES ABOUT 3 1/2 CUPS, OR 6 SERVINGS

ere's a fine sandwich, reminiscent of the sea. The tofu is baked to tender breaded perfection, and the lemony tartar sauce is just right.

The impetus for this invention was owner Bob Goldberg's craving for a childhood favorite: fish sticks. I think he did them one better.

Filet of Soul (Tofu Filet)

1 pound firm tofu

$^2/_3$ cup fine, dry, whole wheat bread crumbs

2 tablespoons whole wheat pastry flour

$^3/_4$ teaspoon onion powder

$^1/_2$ teaspoon sea salt

$^1/_2$ teaspoon kelp granules (available at natural food stores)

Safflower oil

TARTAR SAUCE

$^1/_3$ cup Vegenaise or eggless mayonnaise

4 teaspoons sweet pickle relish

1 teaspoon freshly squeezed lemon juice

$^1/_4$ teaspoon cream of tartar

4 whole wheat sesame seed burger buns

Vegenaise or eggless mayonnaise for burger buns (optional)

4 leaves butter or red leaf lettuce, washed and dried

Lemon wedges

Preheat oven to 375°F.

Rinse tofu, then slice lengthwise into 4 thin slices so that you get the widest, longest pieces possible (each slice will nicely cover a sesame seed bun, with tofu to spare). Dry slices thoroughly on towels.

In a wide, flat bowl or pan, mix together the bread crumbs, flour, onion powder, salt, and kelp. Pour a little oil into a bowl and, using a pastry brush, coat the tofu slices with oil, then dip into the breading mix, coating tofu thoroughly.

Transfer to an oiled baking sheet, and bake for about 10 minutes on first side; turn over and bake an additional 7 to 10 minutes, or until nicely browned.

To make tartar sauce: Mix together Vegenaise, relish, lemon juice, and cream of tartar. Set aside.

Toast burger buns in the hot oven briefly until slightly crisp. Spread on a little Vegenaise if desired. Place tofu filets on bottom buns, top with generous spoonfuls of tartar sauce, lettuce leaves, a squeeze or two of lemon from the lemon wedge, and cover with top buns. Serve right away.

MAKES 4 SANDWICHES

You can buy ready-made versions of this salad at any natural food store, but I like it fresh. It takes all of about five minutes to mix up a batch of this for lunch.

You can adjust the seasonings to your taste, and it keeps well in the fridge for several days. Celery salt, pickle juice, lemon, and mustard add pizzazz. Turmeric powder is often added to tofu salad for that "eggy" color, but I prefer the sweeter taste without it. This one's a little different than the one we currently sell at Follow Your Heart, which does contain turmeric.

Tofu Salad (Eggless Egg salad)

10 ounces firm or extra-firm fresh tofu

1 cup diced celery (about 2 large stalks)

$1/4$ cup Vegenaise or eggless mayonnaise

1 tablespoon sweet pickle juice (save from jar of sweet pickles)

2 teaspoons Dijon mustard

1 teaspoon celery salt

1 teaspoon freshly squeezed lemon juice

Using your hands, crumble tofu into a bowl. Add celery, Vegenaise, pickle juice, mustard, celery salt, and lemon juice and mix thoroughly but gently. Adjust seasonings to taste. Serve as a sandwich filling or on a bed of greens.

MAKES 3 TO 4 SERVINGS

Not the least bit fishy, and it's dolphin safe.

Follow Your Heart has had a few versions of mock tuna salad over the years. This one came from Marsha Stamp, my old friend and former kitchen manager extraordinaire.

Marsha was always inventing delightful things to eat, and when she didn't feel like cooking, would seek out someone else's wonderful food. Before we started work on Saturdays, we'd meet at Follow Your Heart in the Valley, then drive over to west Los Angeles for pastries and coffee at Michel Richard's, an inspired French bakery. A long trek, but well worth it. We'd drive back, full of croissants, ready to cook and serve *our* customers the rest of the day.

Happy Tuna

1^1/$_2$ cups raw cashew pieces

1 cup rolled oats

^{1}/$_2$ cup raw sunflower seeds

^{3}/$_4$ cup water

^{1}/$_4$ cup minced onion

6 tablespoons minced celery

5 tablespoons minced green bell pepper

^{1}/$_4$ cup Vegenaise or eggless mayonnaise

1^1/$_2$ tablespoons freshly squeezed lemon juice

1 tablespoon tamari soy sauce

Sea salt

Place cashews, oats, and sunflower seeds in the bowl of a food processor fitted with the steel blade, and process 20 seconds, or until a slightly chunky meal is formed. Pour into a medium bowl along with the water, onion, celery, bell pepper, Vegenaise, lemon juice, and tamari. Mix thoroughly. Add salt to taste. Use as a sandwich filling or serve on a bed of greens.

MAKES 2^1/$_2$ CUPS, OR ENOUGH FOR 4 TO 6 SERVINGS

A gorgeous summer sandwich, open-faced, succulent, and tender. It might seem a little odd—a sandwich made of cornbread and vegetables, but think of it as a polenta pizza. If that doesn't help, just trust me. This looks so good you'll want to dive in.

Roasted Eggplant, Leeks, and Italian Cheeses on Cornbread

Olive oil

2 large eggplants (about 2^1/$_2$ pounds), sliced ^{3}/$_8$ inch thick

4 large leeks (about 1 pound)

4 ounces mozzarella cheese, grated

4 ounces provolone cheese, grated

1 recipe Moist Oatmeal Cornbread (page 34), cut into 6 squares and halved horizontally (You will only need 4 of the squares for this recipe; save the extra 2 pieces for another use, such as breakfast.)

1 small bunch basil, washed, stemmed, and torn into large pieces

Fresh garden tomatoes as garnish, in season (optional)

Preheat oven to 350°F.

Brush a little oil evenly over 2 large baking sheets. Using about 4 tablespoons oil, brush both sides of eggplant slices and lay them closely together on the baking sheets. Bake for about 25 minutes, or until undersides are browned; turn pieces and bake for about another 20 minutes. Both sides of eggplant should be lightly browned and a little crisp. Remove slices to a platter.

To wash leeks thoroughly: Trim and discard tough green parts, keeping a couple inches of green, and remove roots at stem. Make a long slice lengthwise down the leek, cutting just three quarters of the way through. Rinse leek under running water until all traces of sand and dirt are gone. Cut this way, the leek will stay together but it is easy to clean. Repeat with remaining leeks. Slice cleaned leeks into rounds about ^{1}/$_2$ inch thick. In a large frying pan, sauté leeks over medium heat in about 2 tablespoons oil, stirring often, until leeks are very tender, 15 to 20 minutes. Remove from heat.

MIX mozzarella and provolone cheeses together.

TO make sandwiches, lay 8 halved cornbread slices on a large baking sheet. Distribute the leeks evenly on the cornbread, then the eggplant slices on top of leeks (about 2 eggplant slices per square), the basil, and the cheese mixture. Bake for about 5 minutes, or just until cheese melts. Serve 2 pieces per serving, with tomato slices to garnish each plate, if desired.

variation To make this dish more elegant—and perhaps elevate it to the status of a main dish—you could ladle 3 or 4 ounces of Simple Tomato Sauce (page 129) on individual plates, and set a sandwich on it.

MAKES 4 SERVINGS

I love this sandwich: the bread, rich with whole wheat flavor, the Italian cheeses, the sweet surprise of shredded carrots, tangy red onion, and crisp romaine. It's guaranteed to be the most beautiful sub you've ever eaten, filled with a rainbow of color.

Submarine Sandwich

1 whole wheat submarine sandwich bun, about 8 inches long or an equal section of a baguette or a Mexican *boleo* (preferably a soft, not crusty loaf)

Vegenaise or eggless mayonnaise

Dijon mustard

2 to 3 ounces thinly sliced provolone, Swiss, or mozzarella cheese, preferably imported (or use a combination)

2 large slices ripe tomato

2 thin slices sweet red onion

1 small carrot, grated (fine holes make long shreds; this is preferred)

About $1/2$ cup shredded romaine lettuce

3 or 4 pepperoncinis

Italian Dressing (page 70)

Wrap bread in foil and place in a 300°F oven for just a few minutes, or until it's heated through. Remove foil, and slice bun almost in half horizontally, leaving the top and bottom connected along one side. Spread one half generously with Vegenaise, the other lightly with mustard. Layer the cheeses on bottom half, alternating if different kinds are used, then build up: tomatoes next, then the onion, carrot shreds, lettuce, pepperoncinis, and a little Italian dressing, to taste. Cut in half diagonally and serve.

MAKES 1 LARGE SANDWICH, OR 1 OR 2 SERVINGS

Because it is dense and chewy, tempeh makes a great taco or burrito filling. You can of course vary the flavors here with your own favorite spices and a variety of salsas. You could also add grated cheese to the tacos right before serving.

Tempeh Tacos

2 tablespoons olive oil

1 large onion, chopped

12 ounces plain tempeh, crumbled into large pieces (I like Surata Soyfoods Co-op Original Tempeh, available at natural food stores)

1 tablespoon tamari soy sauce

1 teaspoon ground cumin

12 corn tortillas, wrapped in foil

1/2 to 1 cup coarsely chopped fresh cilantro

2 cups crisp shredded lettuce, such as romaine

About 1/4 cup salsa, red or green

Preheat oven to 350°F.

In a large skillet, heat the oil and sauté the onion over medium-high heat, stirring often, for about 5 minutes, or until onion is browned around the edges and fragrant. Add tempeh, tamari, and cumin; reduce heat to medium and stir until tempeh is slightly browned, about 3 minutes. Turn off heat, adjust seasonings to taste, and cover to keep warm.

Meanwhile, warm tortillas in oven until they are soft and pliable. Fold each tortilla in half, and spoon in the tempeh mixture; top with cilantro, lettuce, and salsa and serve immediately.

MAKES 12 TACOS, OR 4 TO 6 SERVINGS

There is cheddar, and then there is cheddar. The cheese I'm talking about here is sharp, really sharp, aged 2 or 3 years, from New York, Canada, or England, where they know how to make it.

This is the sandwich's equivalent to a slice of warm apple pie, served with a nice slice of cheddar on top. It is fresh and tart, with the ravishing shades of green apple and watercress.

The Apple Cheddar Watercress Sandwich

2 slices whole wheat bread

Vegenaise or eggless mayonnaise

6 large sprigs watercress, stemmed

2 round slices tart green apple (such as Pippin or Granny Smith), cored, unpeeled

Sharp cheddar cheese, sliced (enough to cover a slice of bread with 1 layer)

Spread bread with Vegenaise to taste, arrange watercress on bottom slice of bread, top with apple, then cheese, then bread again. Slice diagonally and serve!

MAKES 1 SERVING

old the corned beef. Use bako bits or wheatmeat with delicious results (I prefer bako bits because they have more oomph).

This is such a good sandwich: melted Swiss cheese, sauerkraut, mustard, and crispy bread. You've got to have a great rye—one that will give you large slices and a chewy crust.

The Reuben Sandwich

2 large slices rye bread, like corn-rye or sourdough rye

Vegenaise or eggless mayonnaise

Mustard, preferably Gulden's

2 tablespoons vegetarian bako bits (such as Fakin' Bacon Bits) or several thin slices wheatmeat* (enough to cover bread in a single layer)

$1^1/2$ cups sauerkraut (squeeze to drain and discard liquid, yielding about 1 cup)

2 thin slices Swiss cheese, approximately $3^1/2$ by 4 inches

Sliced dill pickles

RUSSIAN DRESSING

$2/3$ cup Vegenaise or eggless mayonnaise

$1/4$ cup ketchup

1 tablespoon sweet pickle relish

Preheat oven to 350°F.

Spread 1 slice of bread lightly with Vegenaise, the other with mustard. Sprinkle bako bits or place wheatmeat on top of the mustard side, then arrange sauerkraut on top of this. Layer on the cheese (slices will overlap slightly) to cover sauerkraut. Place both sandwich halves (the Vegenaised side is still plain) on a baking sheet, and bake for several minutes, just until cheese melts. (Check on the Vegenaised slice: Once it is lightly toasted, you may need to take it out before the other side is done.) Remove from oven.

*Wheatmeat, also known by its Japanese name—seitan—is available fresh or frozen in natural food stores. It comes in various flavors made to imitate meat: Get a beef style if available. Thaw first if frozen. Also, as of this writing, Follow Your Heart's deli carries wheatmeat pastrami, which we use in the restaurant. You can purchase it at the store, and we will also ship it. Contact us by phone or through our Web site.

Meanwhile, make the Russian Dressing: Stir together Vegenaise, ketchup, and relish. Makes just under 1 cup. (Refrigerate any unused dressing.)

On top of the cheese, arrange dill pickles and add a generous drizzle of Russian Dressing. Top with other slice of toasted rye and cut sandwich in half. Serve immediately.

MAKES 1 SERVING

*I*ts power is its simplicity: This soup is the essence of autumn. Smooth and creamy, it has no added cream. Mushroom stock adds rich flavor.

Butternut Squash Soup

3 pounds butternut squash

4 tablespoons ($^1/_2$ stick) sweet butter

$^1/_2$ cup chopped yellow onion

4 cups Mushroom Stock (page 107)

Sea salt

Freshly ground black pepper

$^1/_4$ cup chopped fresh parsley

Cut the squash into 4 to 6 large pieces. Remove the seeds and peel off the skin. (You will need a sturdy, wide peeler for this job.) Cut the squash into 1-inch pieces and set aside.

In a heavy-bottomed 3- to 4-quart soup pot, melt the butter. Add the onion and sauté for 5 minutes over low heat, stirring frequently, until onion is barely translucent. Add the squash pieces and continue to cook, stirring occasionally, for about 15 minutes. Add the Mushroom Stock and bring the soup to a boil; reduce heat and simmer, covered, about 15 minutes, or until squash is very tender.

Puree soup in a food processor, blender, or through the small holes of a food mill. (Be careful—mixture is quite hot. You may want to let it cool slightly before pureeing.)

Return soup to pot and reheat slightly. Add salt and pepper to taste. Serve, garnished with parsley.

MAKES 4 TO 6 SERVINGS

Cream of Broccoli is one of Follow Your Heart's most popular soups. Our own Kathy Goldberg created it; it's comfort food, and easy to prepare. Half-and-half makes it creamy, but not overly rich. Broccoli is front and center.

Cream of Broccoli Soup

1 bunch broccoli (about 2 pounds)

6 cups Mushroom Stock (page 107) or vegetable stock

1 large potato, peeled and chopped (about 1 1/2 cups)

1 large stalk celery, chopped

1 medium leek, thinly sliced (1 cup)

1 small bay leaf

1 cup half-and-half

Sea salt

Freshly ground black pepper

Chopped fresh chives

Cut the stems off the broccoli, and cut them into small pieces. Break the tops of the broccoli into small florets, and set aside.

In a 4-quart saucepan, combine the stock, broccoli stems, potato, celery, leek, and bay leaf. Bring to a boil, reduce heat, cover partially, and simmer steadily for about 35 minutes, until the vegetables are very tender. Remove the bay leaf.

Add the broccoli florets and continue cooking about 10 minutes, or until florets are just tender. Add half-and-half. Season with salt and pepper, and adjust seasonings to taste. Serve, garnished with chopped chives.

variation You may also puree the soup if you like a smooth texture. Or puree just half of it and mix it back in with the rest. If you do this, let mixture cool slightly before pureeing.

MAKES 4 TO 6 SERVINGS

An Italian-style classic: Simple peasant ingredients combine to make a fabulous winter soup. The recipe comes from Kristine McCallister, a talented artist and former Follow Your Heart chef. Besides telling the best jokes, Kristine has a gift for naming soups. To honor the Beatles, she served "Let it Bean" and "Give Peas a Chance." When the Lakers beat the Celtics back in the 1980s, there was "Cream of Abdul in a Jar." Great things happen when you turn artists loose in the kitchen.

This tastes great served with a loaf of crusty bread and Italian olives or olive spread.

Great Northern Beans and Greens Soup

14 ounces dried Great Northern beans or other mild white beans, such as cannellini, soaked overnight in water to cover

1 1/2 to 2 quarts vegetable or Mushroom Stock (page 107)

1 pound Swiss chard, preferably the ruby variety, stemmed

Sea salt

1/3 cup extra-virgin olive oil

1 large onion, finely chopped (1 1/4 cups)

6 medium cloves garlic, minced

Three 3-inch sprigs fresh rosemary, stemmed and coarsely chopped

4 ounces tubetti or other short tubular pasta (preferably imported)

Freshly ground black pepper

1 tablespoon Bragg's Liquid Aminos* (optional)

1/4 cup freshly grated imported Parmesan cheese (optional)

Drain and discard soaking water from beans and place beans in a 5-quart pot with stock or water—liquid should cover beans by about 2 inches. Bring to a boil, then reduce heat to low and simmer, partially covered, until beans are tender, 1 to 1 1/2 hours.

*Bragg's Liquid Aminos, a soy-based liquid seasoning, add flavor, especially if a mild vegetable stock is used; if using the mushroom stock, you probably won't need the added Aminos.

Meanwhile, wash and trim chard and place in another 5-quart pot with very little water, and about 1 teaspoon salt. Cover, bring to a boil reduce heat and simmer until tender and still bright green, about 7 minutes. Drain and reserve liquid for soup stock. Set chard aside to cool; when cool, chop coarsely.

Heat oil in a large skillet over medium heat. Add onions, garlic, and rosemary, stirring frequently, until onions are golden. Remove onions, garlic, and rosemary with a slotted spoon and set aside, reserving as much oil as possible in the pan. Add drained and chopped chard to the pan and stir to coat with oil. Set aside.

When beans are tender, add onions, garlic, and rosemary to the pot. Also add liquid from cooking chard, and enough stock to restore the liquid to about 2 inches above beans, approximately 3 cups.

Bring soup to a boil, add pasta, and cook until it is al dente, about 10 minutes. Add chard with its oil, salt and pepper to taste, and the Bragg's Liquid Aminos, if using.

Stir and serve with optional Parmesan.

MAKES 6 TO 8 SERVINGS

*C*eci (pronounced che-chee) means "chickpeas" in Italian. A hearty, simple soup, perfect for chilly fall and winter days. Have extra vegetable stock on hand if you plan to reheat it, as it will continue to thicken.

Pasta e Ceci

1/4 cup olive oil

1/2 cup chopped onion

2 cloves garlic, minced

1 teaspoon chopped fresh rosemary

1/4 teaspoon dried sage

One 28-ounce can Italian plum tomatoes, with juice

One 15-ounce can chickpeas, drained (about 1 1/2 cups) or freshly cooked chickpeas

2 cups water or vegetable stock

4 ounces small pasta for soup (tubetti, ditalini, or small shells)

Sea salt

Freshly ground black pepper

Fresh Italian (flat-leafed) parsley sprigs

Freshly grated Pecorino Romano or Parmigiano-Reggiano cheese

Pour oil into a 3½-quart saucepan over medium heat. Add onion, and cook, stirring occasionally for a few minutes, or until onion is golden. Add garlic, rosemary, and sage, and continue cooking and stirring until the garlic is colored a pale gold. Add tomatoes and their juice, and cook, uncovered, stirring occasionally for about 10 minutes.

Add chickpeas and cook for 5 minutes. Remove pot from heat. Puree most of the soup, about three-quarters of it, through the large holes of a food mill into a bowl (or use a food processor); add puree back to soup in the pot, along with the water. Place over medium heat.

Stir occasionally as the soup returns to a boil. When it does, add the pasta and cover the pot. Lower heat to a simmer and cook the soup, covered, until the pasta is just al dente. Add salt and pepper to taste, a little more water or stock if it seems too thick, and serve, sprinkled with parsley sprigs and grated cheese.

MAKES 4 TO 6 SERVINGS

I love this easy soup, and if I'm not feeling well it's the first thing I think of. Because it's quick, I can usually muster up the energy to cook it, and the ingredients are basic staples in the vegetable drawer and pantry. It's also great, leftover, for breakfast (like they do in Japan).

You could embellish this soup with leftover rice or soba noodles (fine, thin Japanese noodles that sometimes have buckwheat added). Cook the noodles separately, and add some to your serving bowl before ladling in the hot soup.

Simple Miso Soup

1 tablespoon safflower oil

1 small onion, quartered and thinly sliced

1 large carrot, sliced diagonally $1/4$ inch thick

3 cups water

Four $1/4$-inch-thick slices fresh ginger

$1/2$ small head cabbage, halved and thinly sliced

4 teaspoons brown rice (*genmai*) miso OR 2 teaspoons *hatcho* miso with 2 teaspoons sweet white miso (see Glossary, page 187)

Tamari soy sauce

4 ounces firm tofu, cut into $1/2$-inch cubes (optional)

In a large saucepan, heat oil over medium heat; add onion and sauté 5 minutes, stirring occasionally, until onion is barely translucent. Add carrot and sauté, stirring occasionally, for 5 more minutes, or until carrot is a little browned and fragrant. Add water and ginger and bring to a boil. Reduce heat and simmer for 5 minutes, or until carrot is tender; add cabbage and simmer 5 more minutes, until cabbage is just tender. Turn off heat. Dissolve miso with 1 or 2 tablespoons of the hot soup broth; add this back to soup. Add tamari or more miso, to taste. Add tofu, if desired. Serve immediately.

MAKES 2 TO 3 SERVINGS

note This soup is better for you if it isn't reheated. Once the miso is heated to boiling, the favorable bacteria in the miso are killed. It will still taste delicious leftover, but it isn't a soup to stockpile in the freezer—that's why I've made such a small amount.

This soup is summer personified. It must be made with very fresh, preferably just picked, corn on the cob. It is unbelievably sweet, and sumptuously creamy, without cream. It is adapted from a recipe by Alice Waters of Chez Panisse (via the old *Cook's* magazine), a master at using what is seasonal and fresh. So simple, yet so good.

After the soup is pureed, you can strain it through a medium-holed sieve to make it really smooth, though I like the thicker texture of it with the corn kernel skins left in.

Choose either the sweet Tomato-Basil or Spicy Tomato-Jalapeño Salsa (see below), depending on your mood and the rest of your meal. Garnished with Spicy Tomato-Jalapeño Salsa, this would be a delightful opener for Enchiladas Verde (page 112). Garnished with Tomato-Basil Salsa, serve it as an opener for one of the pasta entrees.

Sweet Corn Velvet Soup

6 large, very fresh ears white or yellow corn (yielding about 3 3/4 cups cut kernels)

2 tablespoons unsalted butter

Sea salt

Freshly ground white pepper

3 cups water

TOMATO-BASIL SALSA

1 medium, ripe tomato, chopped

Several large fresh basil leaves, chopped

SPICY TOMATO-JALAPEÑO SALSA

1 medium, ripe tomato, chopped

1 tablespoon finely chopped fresh cilantro

1/2 to 1 jalapeño pepper, minced

Husk corn and cut kernels into a bowl with a sharp knife, saving any juice. Then, with a dull knife, scrape the cobs of corn of any remaining pulp or juice, adding all of this to the rest of corn in bowl.

In a 3- or 4-quart heavy saucepan, melt butter. Add corn and a little salt and pepper to taste. Stir frequently over medium heat for 2 or 3 minutes. Add water;

bring to a boil, then reduce heat and simmer, uncovered, stirring occasionally, for 15 minutes.

While the soup is cooking, prepare your choice of salsa: stir together tomato and basil, with salt and pepper to taste OR tomato and cilantro with jalapeño to taste. Set aside.

When soup is done, remove from heat and allow to cool slightly. Pour soup into a food processor fitted with the steel blade, and process until smooth. Taste the soup and see if you like the texture. If you'd like it smoother pour soup through a medium-holed sieve to strain out the corn kernel skins. (A very fine strainer won't work here—the liquid will be hard to pass through.) In either case, then pour the soup back into the pot, and heat just until hot. Pour into individual bowls, then garnish with a dollop of salsa. Serve immediately.

MAKES 4 SERVINGS

Tom Kha Kai, the chicken and coconut milk soup served at many Thai restaurants, was this soup's inspiration. Tofu takes the place of chicken, and mushrooms and fresh mushroom stock give it a full and almost meaty flavor.

If you can obtain fresh lemongrass at an Asian market or well-stocked grocery, your soup will be all the more authentic, but lemon rind works well, too. If you do use lemongrass, make sure it is very fresh (bright green), and do not attempt to chew it—rather, let the pieces gather in the bottom of your bowl. It is tough, and is used for its flavor and color only. Lastly, if at all possible, use shiitake and oyster mushrooms. These mushrooms are distinctive, delicious, and downright interesting.

Thai Coconut-Mushroom Soup

4 cups Mushroom Stock (page 107)

One 14-ounce can coconut milk

4 ounces fresh shiitake mushrooms (or regular mushrooms), sliced in large pieces (if using shiitakes, discard stems—they're tough)

4 ounces fresh oyster mushrooms, sliced in large pieces (If fresh are unavailable, use $1/2$ ounce dried oyster mushrooms soaked in 1 cup lukewarm water for $1/2$ hour. Strain liquid and add to soup; wash mushrooms, and slice into large pieces.)

4 ounces firm tofu, cut into 1-inch cubes

3 stalks fresh lemongrass, sliced into 1-inch pieces (about $3/4$ cup) or $1 1/2$ teaspoons grated lemon peel (yellow part only)

$1/2$ cup chopped green onions

$1/4$ cup finely chopped fresh cilantro

$1/4$ cup freshly squeezed lemon juice

Scant $1/2$ teaspoon crushed red pepper flakes

Tamari soy sauce or sea salt

Combine the stock, coconut milk, and mushrooms in a large pot and bring to a boil. Reduce heat to simmer; add tofu and lemongrass and simmer, uncovered, 10 to 15 minutes, or until mushrooms are just tender (shiitake mushrooms will still be a little firm; that's ok). Add onions, cilantro, lemon juice, pepper flakes, and tamari to taste. Serve immediately.

MAKES 4 SERVINGS

Full, rich, and (dare I say) meaty flavor distinguishes this vegetarian stock. It puts canned vegetable broth to shame. A great alternative to beef stock in soups and risottos, it is the base for our Thai Coconut-Mushroom Soup (page 106) and our Risotto with Porcini Mushrooms (page 125). It will lend itself to many other recipes as well.

Mushroom Stock

8 cups water

2¹/₂ cups chopped yellow onion (2 medium onions)

2 pounds mushrooms, minced (use food processor)

1 tablespoon freshly squeezed lemon juice

2 teaspoons sea salt

In a large stock pot, combine water, onions, mushrooms, lemon juice, and salt. Bring to a boil, then reduce heat to simmer for 1¹/₄ hours, partially covered. Allow to cool. Strain through a fine sieve or through a double thickness of cheesecloth that has been rinsed, then squeezed dry. Store, refrigerated, for up to 3 days or freeze for up to 2 months.

MAKES 8 CUPS

Entrees

When I need to make a fast dinner, this is one I often turn to. The ingredients are easy to keep on hand, it's simple, and kids love it and can help with the preparation.

You can vary the toppings, type of salsa, even the beans (for example, use pintos instead of black beans) according to what your family likes. You could make our Spanish Rice (page 79) or brown rice instead of white, if you have extra time. You could omit the cheese and yogurt if you don't eat dairy products, and use extra salsa and guacamole instead. Let the kids build their own, just the way they like it!

Black Bean Tostadas (or Burritos), in 20 minutes

3 cups water

1 1/2 cups white basmati rice

1 tablespoon butter or margarine

Pinch of sea salt

2 tablespoons olive oil

Two 15-ounce cans organic whole black beans

2 teaspoons ground cumin

2 teaspoons tamari soy sauce

8 ounces cheddar or jack cheese, shredded (optional)

2 medium tomatoes, chopped

1/2 large head romaine lettuce, cut in fine shreds

1 cucumber, peeled and chopped

1 avocado, sliced (or mash and season with a little salsa and tomatoes, to taste)

1/2 bunch fresh cilantro, finely chopped

Salsa, fresh or bottled, red or green

1 small can sliced olives (optional)

8 ounces plain yogurt or sour cream (optional)

12 large (8- to 10-inch) whole wheat tortillas or chapatis (for burritos), or 12 corn tortillas (for tostadas)

In a medium saucepan, bring to a boil water, rice, butter, and salt. Lower heat and simmer for 15 to 20 minutes, covered, until rice is fluffy and all water absorbed. Meanwhile, heat oil in a large, heavy skillet. Add beans and their liquid, cumin, and tamari. Simmer gently, stirring occasionally, until most of the liquid is gone. Turn off heat and cover to keep warm. (You can mash the beans if you prefer a refried texture.)

Preheat oven to 300°F. While beans are heating, prepare other ingredients as listed, and arrange them on a large platter or cutting board. Heat the flour tortillas in the oven, uncovered on a baking sheet, several stacked up together, until warm but still soft; for corn tortillas, spread tortillas in a single layer and heat for just a few minutes, until slightly crisp. Or you can toast the corn tortillas on a gas stove by laying them over a cast-iron flame tamer, with the flame on low, just until crisp, 1 to 2 minutes.

For tostadas, place a thin layer of beans on a crisp tortilla, top with rice, then some shredded cheese; add lettuce, tomatoes, cucumber, and avocado or guacamole; sprinkle with cilantro, salsa, yogurt, and olives. For burritos, place about $^1/_3$ cup cooked beans in a line down the middle of each warm tortilla. Top with a little rice, cheese, and anything else you like (except lettuce) fold top and bottom edges toward beans, then roll in the sides. You can serve the lettuce on the side topped with salsa, yogurt, and avocado, or a little salad dressing.

MAKES 4 TO 6 SERVINGS

Tempted by tempeh? I wish cooks would use it more; it bears exploration. With its mild, nutty flavor and meaty texture, tempeh inspires these flavorful enchiladas. Serve with a colorful salad and a piquant dressing.

Enchiladas Verde

One 14$\frac{1}{2}$-ounce can or about 2 cups mushroom or flavorful vegetable stock (see Mushroom Stock, page 107)

12 ounces (1$\frac{1}{2}$ cups) mild tomatillo salsa*

1 bunch spinach (about 1 pound), washed thoroughly and stemmed

1 to 2 tablespoons olive oil

1 medium onion, chopped

12 ounces plain, unseasoned tempeh (such as Surata Soyfoods Co-op), crumbled into small pieces

Sea salt

Freshly ground black pepper

6 ounces mild creamy goat cheese

12 corn tortillas

4 ounces grated Swiss cheese or other flavorful white cheese

$\frac{1}{2}$ cup chopped fresh cilantro

Preheat oven to 400°F. Oil a 9-by-13-inch Pyrex baking dish or equivalent.

Place stock and salsa in a medium saucepan. Bring to a boil, then reduce to a simmer and continue cooking, uncovered, for about 15 minutes, or until sauce thickens slightly. Cover and set aside.

With water still clinging to the leaves, place spinach in a pot large enough to hold all of it, and cook over medium heat, covered, until it is wilted and most of the liquid is gone, about 10 minutes. Drain and allow to cool. When cooled, squeeze the spinach until thoroughly dry, and chop coarsely. Set aside.

*A Note about salsas: I like to use Trader Joe's Salsa Verde, which comes in 12-ounce jars, or Herdez Salsa Verde, available in 6-ounce cans in many supermarkets. You can also use a fresh salsa verde, but they tend to be spicier.

In a skillet, heat the oil over medium heat, and add the onion. Cook, stirring often, for about 5 minutes, until onion is translucent. Stir in crumbled tempeh. Continue cooking, stirring occasionally, for about 3 minutes, or until tempeh is lightly browned, adding more oil if necessary. Season with salt and pepper. Remove from heat.

To assemble the enchiladas: On a countertop near your stove, arrange the spinach, sautéed onions and tempeh, and the goat cheese and tortillas. Bring the stock mixture to the barest simmer. Dip a tortilla* in the sauce and hold there for about 10 seconds, or until it softens slightly. (If the tortilla is dipped in the hot stock mixture too long, it'll fall apart; not long enough, and it will crack when you roll it.) Take it out, lay flat on a board or counter, and fill it across the middle with the tempeh mixture, some spinach, and a spoonful of goat cheese. Roll up tightly and place seam side down in the casserole. Repeat until all 12 are rolled and placed into pan. (I place 8 enchiladas lengthwise down the pan, and in the remaining space I place the other 4 enchiladas, 2 by 2, widthwise.)

Pour remaining sauce over the rolled tortillas. Top with grated Swiss cheese. Bake for 10 to 15 minutes, uncovered, until cheese is melted and sauce is bubbling. Serve immediately, garnished with cilantro.

MAKES 4 TO 6 SERVINGS

*Corn tortillas have a right side and a wrong side. The right side is the way it naturally curls: When you lay a tortilla on a flat surface, notice which way it is starting to curl—that's the same direction you want to roll. Also, manufactured tortillas have lines running across them, and when you lay the tortilla in front of you, ready to roll from bottom to top, make sure those lines are running from left to right. If not, the tortillas will break when you roll them.

Why is the chicken happy? Because it's *still* crossing the road.

This is hearty comfort food. It's a one-dish meal, but you could add a simple salad or sautéed greens.

Wheatmeat and seitan are products made from wheat gluten, the protein derived from wheat with the starch removed. Seitan is a traditional Japanese food, but is not very well known here except in the vegetarian and Asian communities. It is usually seasoned with tamari and ginger. Wheatmeat is wheat gluten with flavors added to resemble meat. Both have a chewy texture and are high in protein. They are readily available in the refrigerator section of natural food stores, located near the tofu. Sometimes these products can be found in the freezer section as well.

Happy Chicken Pot Pie

$^1/_3$ cup olive oil

1 large carrot, diced small (about $^3/_4$ cup)

1 medium yellow onion, chopped (about 1 cup)

1 teaspoon chopped fresh rosemary

2 cups seasoned seitan or wheatmeat, "chicken style" or regular, chopped into $^3/_4$-inch pieces

1$^1/_2$ cups frozen corn, rinsed with warm water to thaw

1 cup frozen peas, rinsed with warm water to thaw

2 teaspoons Morga Instant Vegetable Broth Mix (available at natural food stores)

1 teaspoon sea salt

$^1/_2$ teaspoon dried thyme

$^1/_2$ teaspoon dried dill

$^1/_4$ teaspoon freshly ground black pepper

Pinch of freshly grated nutmeg

2 tablespoons flour + extra for rolling dough

1 tablespoon arrowroot powder or cornstarch

1$^1/_4$ cups water

1 recipe Nutty Pie Crust (page 159), slightly chilled but soft enough to roll out

In a large skillet (large enough to hold all ingredients except crust), heat oil over medium heat. Sauté carrot, onion, and rosemary until carrots are tender and onions translucent, stirring frequently, about 10 minutes. Turn off heat. Stir in the seitan, corn, peas, Morga powder, salt, thyme, dill, pepper, and nutmeg. Stir and allow everything to introduce itself to everything else.

In a small bowl, whisk flour and arrowroot powder into the water until smooth and all lumps are gone. (Or you may mix these in a blender container until smooth). Stir this into the skillet with everything else; heat to a simmer, and cook for about 2 minutes, stirring occasionally, until mixture has thickened slightly. Turn off heat and set aside.

Preheat oven to 350°F. Prepare baking dish and pie crust: Divide dough in half, and roll out each half on a floured board into two 10-inch circles about ⅛ inch thick. Place 1 circle of dough in a 9-inch deep-dish pie pan, pressing into bottom rim and letting outer edge fall over sides. Spoon filling into shell, then cover with second circle of dough. Press top and bottom crusts together at edges, folding bottom crust over top; using your fingers, make an attractive edge. (You may want to trim away some crust before doing this if you've got more than an inch in places.) Make about 6 slits in a circular pattern on top crust to allow steam to escape during baking. Bake for 55 to 60 minutes, or until nicely browned and fragrant and filling is bubbling hot. Allow to sit for about 20 minutes before serving.

MAKES 6 SERVINGS

A hearty and heart-warming winter meal, serve this with our Sautéed Spinach and Radicchio (page 78) or a dark green salad.

"Kasha" is the word for roasted buckwheat groats. It is a fragrant, flavorful grain that is often overlooked except in the Jewish community, where it is used in such dishes as kasha varnishkes.

When unroasted, the white groats or grain can be cooked with water like oatmeal to make a breakfast cereal. In this recipe, the groats have already been roasted (you buy them that way—if they are a nutty brown color, they've been roasted), and when cooked, make a delicious container for seasoned mashed potatoes with cabbage. (If you want more information about buckwheat, refer to *The Grains Cookbook* by Bert Greene, which is full of buckwheat lore, recipes, and nutrition facts.)

Kasha pie may be further embellished by adding a mushroom gravy, such as Mark's Scrumptious Mushroom Gravy (page 177), or a double recipe of Mushroom-Garlic Sauce (page 74). It is also delicious as is; gravy really is gilding the lily.

Kasha Potato Pie

CRUST

2 cups boiling water

3/4 cup kasha (toasted buckwheat groats; see note, page 118)

1 teaspoon sea salt

4 tablespoons olive oil + extra for greasing dish

1 1/2 pounds leeks, white and green parts washed, trimmed, and chopped into 3/4-inch pieces (about 8 cups)

1 pound mushrooms, chopped

1 1/4 cups finely chopped onions

4 cloves garlic, minced or pressed

1 tablespoon fresh thyme leaves (stemmed)

1/2 cup tahini

1/3 cup tamari soy sauce

FILLING

2 pounds red potatoes, washed and quartered

4 cups shredded green cabbage

$^1/_4$ cup plain or honey soymilk or regular milk

$^1/_4$ cup chopped fresh parsley

6 tablespoons ($^3/_4$ stick) unsalted butter or nonhydrogenated margarine, divided

1 tablespoon finely chopped fresh dill or 1 teaspoon dried

1 tablespoon nutritional yeast flakes*

1 teaspoon sea salt

$^1/_2$ teaspoon onion powder or granulated onion**

To make pie crust: In a small saucepan, combine water, kasha, and salt, stirring. Bring to a boil, then reduce heat to barest simmer and cook, covered, for about 10 minutes, or until kasha is fluffy and all water is absorbed. Remove from heat and set aside.

In a large skillet, heat oil over medium heat and sauté leeks, mushrooms, onions, garlic, and thyme, stirring often, for 8 to 10 minutes, or until vegetables are just tender and volume is reduced by half. (You may need to do this step in 2 batches, depending on size of your skillet.) Stir in tahini and tamari, then add this mixture to the cooked kasha and stir thoroughly. Set aside.

Preheat oven to 375°F.

To make filling: Place potatoes in 4-quart pot with water just to cover. Bring to a boil, then reduce heat and simmer, covered, for about 20 minutes, or until potatoes are tender. Meanwhile, steam cabbage until slightly tender, about 10 minutes. Remove from heat and set aside.

Drain cooked potatoes and, in a large bowl, mash them with the soymilk, parsley, 4 tablespoons of the butter, dill, yeast flakes, salt, and onion powder until smooth. (Do not overmix.) Now you are ready to assemble the pie.

Lightly oil a 9-by-13-by-2-inch casserole dish. Press kasha mixture into the bottom and sides of your pan, making a crust that is about 1 inch thick. This will be visible at the top when the pie is filled; the top should be nicely shaped

*Nutritional yeast flakes are similar to brewer's yeast (a by-product of the beer-making industry), but have a better flavor— a little like cheese. They can be purchased at natural food stores in the vitamin or bulk section.
**I'm not always wild about onion powders because they get an off taste if not extremely fresh. Make sure yours is newly purchased. It should flow freely and be easy to measure. When fresh, onion powder adds intense and full flavor to a dish.

and smooth and should come up to the top of the pan. Distribute the steamed cabbage evenly on top of the kasha crust, to be followed by the seasoned potatoes. Smooth potato mixture, then rake them attractively with a fork. Dot with remaining 2 tablespoons butter, cut in chunks. Place pie in center of oven and bake for about 30 minutes, or until thoroughly hot and crust is beginning to brown. Then turn your oven on to the broil setting (without moving pie to broiler—just keep it in the oven) and continue cooking for 2 to 3 minutes, or until potatoes turn a beautiful golden brown. Let cool 10 minutes before cutting.

note If toasted buckwheat (kasha) is not available, you can purchase raw buckwheat groats and pan-toast your own: Heat a heavy skillet (cast iron is great) to medium-low, add groats, and toast them, stirring often, for about 10 minutes, or until they are evenly browned and very fragrant. If your skillet is not so heavy, you can help the process along by heating 1 tablespoon of a mild vegetable oil before you add the groats, then proceed as above.

MAKES 6 TO 8 SERVINGS

It looks just like the original, with a creamy texture and delicate flavor reminiscent of cheese, thanks to the nutritional yeast, tofu, and rice milk. Follow Your Heart's own Kathy Goldberg developed this for her son David after discovering his allergy to dairy products; of course, macaroni and cheese was one of his favorite foods. He loves this spin-off. More good news—this recipe doubles very nicely.

Macaroni and No Cheese

$1^1/_2$ tablespoons non-hydrogenated, non-dairy margarine

2 tablespoons unbleached all-purpose flour

2 tablespoons nutritional yeast flakes

$1^1/_2$ teaspoons Morga vegetable broth powder or 1 Morga vegetable bouillon cube, salt added

$1^1/_2$ cups Rice Dream (rice milk), original flavor

1 small clove garlic, minced or pressed

$^1/_2$ teaspoon onion powder

Dash of celery salt

Dash of curry powder

Dash of freshly ground white or black pepper

8 ounces macaroni, ziti, or medium shells

3 ounces firm, fresh tofu

2 teaspoons canola oil

Bring 3 quarts water to a boil.

Meanwhile, prepare the sauce: In a 1-quart saucepan, melt margarine over low heat. Add flour and yeast flakes, and stir until smooth. Cook about 2 minutes, stirring constantly. Add Morga powder and whisk in rice milk, garlic, onion powder, celery salt, curry powder, and pepper. Simmer sauce, uncovered, for 10 to 15 minutes, stirring often, until sauce has thickness of heavy cream. Remove from heat.

Cook pasta in the boiling water until al dente, tender but firm (check package directions for timing). Drain and cover. Keep warm as you finish the recipe.

In a heatproof, variable-speed blender, blend tofu with oil and about $^1/_2$ cup of the sauce. Blend until very smooth, adding more sauce if necessary for blending. Add blended mixture to rest of sauce.

TOSS the hot, drained pasta with the sauce; serve immediately.

MAKES 3 OR 4 KID-SIZED SERVINGS

Mrs. Singh, mother of my friend Jasprit, lives in India and has been a vegetarian all her life. While visiting Santa Barbara, she was kind enough to demonstrate several tantalizing Punjabi dishes while I chopped vegetables and took notes. Afterwards, we sat down to a lunch featuring these flavorful lentils.

To make an Indian feast, serve with Spiced Rice (page 80) with homemade Paneer (Indian cheese, page 82), Indian Spinach with Carrots and Scallions (page 77), and Cilantro and Mint Chutney (page 76).

Mrs. Singh's Red Lentils

1 cup red lentils

2 tablespoons vegetable oil or ghee*

$^1/_2$ cup minced onion

3 large cloves garlic, minced

2 tablespoons minced peeled fresh ginger

4 cups water

$^1/_2$ cup chopped tomatoes

1 teaspoon sea salt

1 teaspoon garam masala** (recipe follows)

1 teaspoon turmeric

$^3/_4$ teaspoon freshly ground black pepper

2 tablespoons chopped fresh cilantro

Wash lentils well: Soak in water to cover for a couple of minutes, drain, and rinse. Repeat 2 more times; drain and set aside.

In a 3- or 4-quart heavy saucepan, heat the oil over medium heat until it is hot but not smoking. Add onion, garlic, and ginger, and cook, stirring often, until

*Ghee is Indian-style clarified butter, which has had all milk solids removed. It can then be stored for a long time at room temperature and used for frying. You can make your own (it's time-consuming—check Indian cookbooks or *The New Joy of Cooking* by Ethan Becker) or you can purchase it at natural food stores and Indian groceries.

**Garam masala* is the name of an Indian spice mixture. It can be purchased at a good spice store or Indian grocery, or make your own. Recipes vary, but the blend I use I learned from cooking teacher and cookbook author Neelam Batra.

onions and garlic are lightly golden, 5 to 7 minutes. Add water, tomatoes, salt, garam masala, turmeric, pepper, and the washed lentils. Bring to a boil, then reduce heat to simmer, and cook, uncovered, 1 to $1^1/_2$ hours. Stir occasionally and add a little more water if necessary. When done, lentils will be almost completely dissolved; a thin liquid will form on top, while a thick puree settles at the bottom. Stir more often toward the end of cooking and keep heat very low to prevent sticking. Garnish with fresh cilantro, and serve.

MAKES 6 TO 8 SERVINGS

Garam Masala

You will need equal amounts by weight of:

Cinnamon sticks

Black peppercorns

Black or green cardamom seeds (if in pods, remove and discard pods, then weigh seeds only)

Cloves

Use a postage scale to weigh spices. One quarter to $^1/_2$ ounce of each spice will make a small batch. Grind in a spice or coffee grinder until a fine powder is formed. Store in cool, dark place. Keeps for 6 to 8 months.

The advertisement read, "Wanted: Vegetarian female to share small house in Northridge. Must love cats." It sounded like me, so I answered it. That was how I met Stacy Wyman, with whom I have shared many meals and recipes, several double-dates, and many meaningful conversations during our college days and beyond. (The conversations continue, mostly via email. Many of them still center around food.)

Stacy gave me the original recipe from which this was adapted. She would probably double the garlic and cheese, however. When we were roommates, she always used more of everything than I did—more cheese on the pizza, more juice from the refrigerator, more soap for the laundry. It became a budget consideration until I laid down the law: We would buy separate groceries and household goods. This allowed us to still be friends.

Most focaccias are topped sparingly, but this one is topped abundantly, even without Stacy doubling it; it is more like a pizza, resulting in a vegetarian entree rather than just bread. Mashed potatoes in the dough make for a moist, tender focaccia; the use of pastry flour helps keep this whole grain, deep-dish crust surprisingly light.

Potato Focaccia

DOUGH

1 tablespoon honey

1 package (2^1/$_4$ teaspoons) active dry yeast

1 cup warm water

1 cup mashed potatoes

2^1/$_2$ cups whole wheat pastry flour

2 cups whole wheat bread flour

2 teaspoons sea salt

^{1}/$_4$ cup extra-virgin olive oil + extra for greasing pan

TOPPING

^{3}/$_4$ cup freshly grated Parmesan cheese (Parmigiano-Reggiano)

^{1}/$_2$ cup extra-virgin olive oil

6 large cloves garlic, minced

^{1}/$_2$ cup chopped green onions

$^1/_4$ cup freshly grated Romano cheese (Pecorino Romano), divided

1 teaspoon dried oregano

1 $^1/_2$ teaspoons dried basil

One 1-pound can whole Italian plum tomatoes, well drained (reserve juice for another use)

Dissolve honey and yeast in warm water, and let stand at room temperature 20 minutes, or until foamy. Meanwhile, place mashed potatoes, both flours, and salt in a food processor fitted with the steel blade. Pulse to mix several times. With machine running, pour in oil and process until mixture resembles coarse crumbs, about 2 minutes. You'll need to turn off machine and mix in ingredients around edges several times.

With machine running, pour yeast mixture through the feed tube. After dough forms a ball, continue processing about 1 minute. Dough will be quite sticky. Scoop dough into a large oiled bowl, and flip over to coat both sides. Cover with a slightly dampened towel and let rise in a warm place, free from drafts, for 45 minutes, or until nearly doubled in bulk.

Preheat oven to 450°F. In a large bowl, mix together the Parmigiano-Reggiano, oil, garlic, onions, 2 tablespoons of the Pecorino Romano, oregano, and basil. When dough has risen, punch down and stretch into a 10-by-14-inch oiled jellyroll pan, building up edges. Let sit 10 minutes.

Spread topping on dough to $^1/_2$ inch of edge. Cut tomatoes in halves or fourths and space evenly across pie. Sprinkle with remaining 2 tablespoons Pecorino Romano. Bake 12 to 15 minutes on lower rack of oven, until edges are golden brown and crisp. Let cool about 10 minutes before serving (olive oil will be absorbed into the crust). Mangia!

MAKES 6 SERVINGS

Mushroom stock has a deep, earthy flavor that adds immeasurably to soups, stews, and risottos. Here, it replaces what would normally be meat stock in a classic Italian recipe. Risotto is Italian comfort food at its best.

Shallots are a mild root vegetable from the onion family. They are small, oblong, and brown-skinned, and the best tasting ones are light purple under the skin. I prefer their mild flavor over onions in this recipe.

Risotto with Porcini Mushrooms

1 scant ounce dried porcini* mushrooms

2 cups lukewarm water

1 quart Mushroom Stock (page 107)

4 tablespoons ($^1/_2$ stick) butter, divided

3 tablespoons olive oil

2 tablespoons finely chopped shallots or yellow onion

2 cups Italian Arborio rice

$^1/_4$ cup freshly grated Parmesan cheese (Parmigiano-Reggiano) + more for grating at table

Sea salt

Freshly ground black pepper

Soak the mushrooms in 2 cups lukewarm water for at least 30 minutes before cooking. After the liquid turns very dark, strain it through a sieve lined with paper towels and add it to the Mushroom Stock. Continue to soak and rinse the mushrooms (dirt clings to them) in frequent changes of water (this water you will discard) until the mushrooms are soft and clean.

Bring the combined mushroom stock to a slow simmer.

In a heavy-bottomed 5-quart saucepan, place 2 tablespoons of the butter and all of the oil over medium-low heat. Sauté the shallots until translucent but not brown, about 5 minutes. Add the rice and stir until it is well coated. Sauté lightly for a few moments and then add about $^1/_2$ cup of the simmering stock.

*Porcini are Italian dried wild mushrooms, available at Italian groceries and many natural food stores and supermarkets.

Stir and continue cooking, until the rice absorbs the liquid; when it begins to dry out, add another $^1/_2$ cup of the simmering stock. It will take about 5 minutes for the liquid to become absorbed. Now add the chopped porcini mushrooms and another $^1/_2$ cup of the mushroom stock. Continue in this manner, adding more stock and stirring each time the last addition of liquid has been absorbed. This process takes about 30 minutes total; the risotto is done when the rice is tender but al dente, firm to the bite. It should not be sticky and pasty, but smooth and a little liquid. When you shake the pan, the risotto will make a wave.

You may not need all of the stock, so don't be in a hurry to use it all up or to add more than $^1/_2$ cup between turns. You might also run out of stock, in which case you can add hot water at the end or another compatible hot vegetable stock (the canned or homemade variety, but not reconstituted bouillon).

When rice is done, turn off heat and mix in the Parmigiano-Reggiano and the remaining 2 tablespoons butter. Taste and add salt, if necessary, and freshly ground pepper. Spoon rice onto a warm serving platter and serve immediately with some more grated Parmigiano-Reggiano on the side.

MAKES 4 TO 6 SERVINGS

uch simpler than a two-crust pie, the cobbler crust is spooned or piped onto the vegetable filling, then quickly baked. Inspired by a recipe in an autumn issue of *Gourmet* magazine, the original called for turkey, but here seitan, flavored wheatmeat, or mushrooms are used instead. Baby limas, carrots, and butternut squash add gorgeous color and sweet flavor.

The filling portion of the pie can be prepared up to one day in advance and kept covered and refrigerated, making life easier for the cook; just bring it to room temperature before adding the crust and baking.

savory vegetable cobbler

FILLING

3 cups water

8 ounces peeled, seeded, butternut squash, cut into $3/4$-inch cubes (about $3/4$ cup)

3 medium carrots, cut in $1^1/2$-inch-thick half circles (about $1^1/4$ cup)

Sea salt

Ice water

$1/2$ cup thawed, frozen baby lima beans

$1/2$ cup thawed frozen petite peas

3 tablespoons unsalted butter + extra for greasing pan

3 tablespoons unbleached all-purpose flour

1 cup Mushroom Stock (page 107) or other vegetable stock

2 tablespoons minced fresh sage

Freshly ground black pepper

5 ounces (about $1/4$ cups) pearl onions, cooked and peeled (see directions for Creamed Onions and Peas, page 174)

18 ounces "chicken-style" wheatmeat or seitan (available in refrigerator section at natural food stores), cut into bite-sized pieces to equal $2^1/2$ cups, OR $1^1/2$ pounds large mushrooms, sliced and sautéed in olive oil or butter for a few minutes, until lightly browned and most of the mushroom juices have evaporated

CRUST

1 1/4 cups unbleached all-purpose flour

1 1/2 teaspoons double-acting baking powder

1/2 teaspoon sea salt

2 tablespoons cold unsalted butter, cut into bits

3/4 cup freshly grated Parmesan cheese (Parmigiano-Reggiano)

1/4 cup freshly grated Romano cheese (Pecorino Romano)

1/2 to 2/3 cup milk or plain soymilk

In a medium saucepan, bring water to a boil; add squash, carrots, and salt to taste, and simmer, uncovered, for 6 to 8 minutes, or until they are just tender. With a slotted spoon, transfer vegetables to a bowl of ice water to stop the cooking. Using the same boiling water, cook the lima beans and peas for about 3 minutes, or until they are just tender. With a slotted spoon, transfer them to the ice water as well, reserving 1 cup of the cooking liquid. When all vegetables are cool, drain in a colander, and set aside.

In a large saucepan, melt the butter over low heat, add the flour, and cook, whisking constantly, for 3 minutes. In a thin stream, slowly whisk in the stock and the reserved cooking liquid; stir in the sage, and salt and pepper to taste. Simmer the sauce, stirring occasionally, for 10 minutes, or until thickened and flavorful. Stir the vegetables into the sauce along with the onions and wheatmeat. Pour into a buttered 1 1/2-quart shallow baking dish.

Preheat oven to 425°F.

For the crust, sift together the flour, baking powder, and salt. With a pastry blender, cut in the butter until mixture resembles coarse meal. Stir in the cheeses, and enough of the milk to form a soft, sticky dough. You can spoon the dough across the top of pie in large dollops, leaving a little space in between, or you can place the dough in a pastry bag fitted with a 3/4-inch star tip, and pipe it around the outside edge of the filling mixture, spiraling toward the center, but leaving the center of the pie uncovered.

Bake in lower third of the oven for 20 to 25 minutes, or until the crust is golden.

MAKES 4 TO 6 SERVINGS

I borrowed the title for this sauce from my sister, Pamela Cook, who sent her version of Simple Tomato Sauce to family members during particularly trying times.

It is good to come home to a pot of simple sauce. Use *only* very ripe, summer tomatoes (nothing else will do) and you will be rewarded with the essence of summer.

I like to enjoy my simple tomato sauce with spaghetti and a simple green salad like Easier Caesar (page 60). Blissfully uncomplicated!

spaghetti with simple Tomato Sauce (for a Complicated World)

2 pounds ripe, sweet tomatoes, halved (quartered if large), unpeeled

1 medium yellow onion, halved

3 tablespoons olive oil

1/2 teaspoon mild honey

Sea salt

1 pound spaghetti (the simplest of pastas) or another shape you enjoy, cooked according to package directions

Grated Parmigiano-Reggiano or Pecorino Romano cheese, the real imported Italian kind (optional)

 Place tomatoes in a medium saucepan. Bring to a boil, then reduce heat to medium and cook, covered, for 10 minutes. Remove from heat.

Using a food mill fitted with a small disk, puree tomatoes into a bowl, discarding skins and seeds.

Place pureed tomatoes back in the saucepan with the onion, oil, and honey. Bring to a boil; reduce heat to low, and simmer, uncovered, for 40 to 50 minutes, or until all traces of raw tomato taste are gone, flavor is nice and savory, and the sauce has thickened slightly (it will still be a fairly thin sauce). Add salt to taste, and discard onion. Toss with hot drained pasta and cheese and serve immediately. Pass extra cheese at the table.

note This sauce can be frozen for 4 to 6 months.

MAKES 6 SERVINGS

A h, the quick dinner. Simple and creamy, this is one of my family's favorites. We always keep mild goat cheese in the refrigerator, and all the other ingredients for this are on hand as well. Serve with a crisp salad or lightly steamed vegetables.

Spaghetti with Garlic and Goat Cheese

3 tablespoons unsalted butter

3 tablespoons extra-virgin olive oil

3 medium cloves garlic, pressed or minced

6 ounces mild, creamy goat cheese

12 ounces spaghetti or medium shells (use imported Italian for best texture)

Parmigiano-Reggiano cheese for grating

In a large pasta pot, bring 6 quarts salted water to a boil.

Meanwhile, prepare sauce: In a heavy skillet, heat butter and oil on low heat. Add garlic and sauté, stirring often, until slightly golden. Remove from heat and add goat cheese. Place back on low heat and stir until cheese melts. Turn off heat and set aside. Add pasta to boiling water; after it returns to a boil, cook uncovered for 1 minute. Turn off heat, cover pot with a folded kitchen towel, then a lid. Let sit for about 5 minutes, or until pasta is al dente, just tender. Drain, reserving a few tablespoons of the pasta water to add to the sauce.

Add as much pasta water to the goat cheese mixture as needed (3 to 4 tablespoons) to make a smooth sauce the texture of thick cream. Add to hot drained pasta and toss. Serve immediately, sprinkled with freshly grated Parmigiano-Reggiano cheese.

MAKES 4 SERVINGS

One of Follow Your Heart's strengths is our diverse multi-ethnic staff. This recipe for Pad Thai was contributed by our cook Sayavath Khantikone, born in Laos. He prefers that we call him Booth, the Laotian word for sun. Booth's road to Follow Your Heart began with a daring swim across a river to escape the repressive regime that had overtaken his country. At one time he had trained to become a monk; he feels that The Heart was his destiny. He contributes many recipes, and abundant joy, to our kitchen.

Quite simple to prepare, actually, yet this dish has complex flavors. I am grateful to Booth for divulging the delightful secrets of making Pad Thai at home.

Pad Thai

4 ounces rice noodles*

1 tablespoon olive or safflower oil + 1 tablespoon extra if using brown rice noodles

2 medium cloves garlic, minced

3 ounces firm tofu, cut into $1/2$-inch cubes

2 tablespoons white wine vinegar

2 tablespoons mild honey

1 tablespoon tamari soy sauce

1 teaspoon paprika

$1^1/2$ cups mung bean sprouts, divided

3 tablespoons ground peanuts, divided

1 tablespoon chopped fresh cilantro

1 green onion, chopped

Crushed red chile peppers

If using brown rice noodles, bring a large pot of water to a boil. Add rice noodles and 1 tablespoon oil and cook until just tender, 8 to 10 minutes (or according to package directions). Drain, rinse with cold water, drain again, and set aside. If using white rice noodles, bring to a boil just enough water to cover

*Use brown rice fettuccine, such as Tinkyada brand, available at natural food stores, or Thai my-tho noodles, made from white rice. The my-tho noodles appear translucent and are available at Asian groceries and some natural food stores.

noodles. Place noodles in a heatproof bowl and pour boiling water over noodles until they are completely covered. Let stand 10 to 15 minutes, or until noodles are just tender. Drain and set aside.

In a large frying pan, place oil over medium heat, and stir-fry garlic until it begins to turn golden, just a minute or two. Add tofu and sauté 2 minutes, stirring often, or until tofu begins to brown. Stir in vinegar, honey, tamari, and paprika. Mix thoroughly, then stir in the rice noodles, 1 cup bean sprouts, and 2 tablespoons ground peanuts. Toss to mix well. Turn off heat. Garnish with remaining bean sprouts and peanuts, cilantro, onion, and chile peppers, to taste. Serve immediately.

MAKES 2 SERVINGS

In September, when fresh basil is at its peak, I buy big bunches of it at the farmer's market and go to work with my food processor. I freeze the pesto in small canning jars (see note below) so we can eat it all winter long. There is nothing like the taste of fresh basil, and even freezing doesn't destroy its vibrant taste (I think the olive oil protects its freshness).

I prefer the flavor of walnuts in this recipe instead of the usual pine nuts. They add body as well as flavor to the sauce.

Pasta with Pesto

3 cups tightly packed basil leaves, stemmed, washed, and spun dry (1 large bunch)

$3/4$ cup extra-virgin olive oil

2 to 3 cloves garlic, peeled (optional)

3 tablespoons walnuts or pine nuts

$3/4$ teaspoon sea salt

1 pound linguine, spaghettini, or orecchiette (pasta shaped like little ears), cooked according to package directions

About $1/3$ cup grated Parmigiano-Reggiano cheese and/or Pecorino Romano

Place basil, oil, garlic, walnuts, and salt in blender container or food processor and blend until smooth. Toss with freshly cooked and drained pasta (you probably won't need all of it—reserve for future use), and top with grated cheese to taste. Or stir the cheese into the pesto first if you wish, then mix with pasta.

note This pesto freezes very well without cheese—cheese won't keep as long in the freezer; just place the mixture in 8-ounce glass canning jars, leaving $1/2$ inch or more headroom, and freeze, for up to several months. To thaw pesto, leave it out for several hours at room temperature, or place in the refrigerator overnight. Add cheese when serving.

MAKES ABOUT $1 1/2$ CUPS, OR 4 TO 6 SERVINGS

If you've read a few vegetarian cookbooks, this won't be the first spanakopita recipe you've come across. I wanted to include it because it's a classic vegetarian dish and is always welcome when you take the time to make it. Ours is unique because it's made without eggs, and gives the option of using alternative cheeses.

It's easy to make once you get the hang of it: Arrange to have lots of empty counter space before you start preparation. Delicious with Quinoa Tabbouleh (page 62) or a Greek salad of cucumbers, tomatoes, and olives, drizzled with fragrant olive oil and good wine vinegar.

Spanakopita (Greek Spinach Pie)

Four 10-ounce packages frozen spinach, thawed

14 ounces mild feta cheese, crumbled (use sheep or goat's milk feta)

8 ounces low-fat ricotta cheese (or mild, creamy goat cheese, such as Chavrie)

1 cup chopped green onions

1 tablespoon dried dill or 2 to 3 tablespoons fresh

1 teaspoon freshly ground white pepper

Sea salt

8 ounces filo dough ($^1/_2$ package or 10 sheets; sold in freezer section of delis, natural food stores, and supermarkets), thawed

8 tablespoons (1 stick) unsalted butter or non-hydrogenated margarine, melted

If spinach is still frozen, steam until just defrosted; drain and cool. Squeeze gently to remove all excess water, then chop and place in a large bowl. Add the feta, ricotta, onions, dill, pepper, and salt to taste. Set aside.

Preheat oven to 350°F.

Unwrap filo dough and spread on a clean surface. Keep covered with a damp towel while working to prevent filo from drying out. Gently take 1 sheet of filo and layer it in a 9-by-13-inch baking dish, brushing lightly with melted butter (use butter sparingly, especially in the beginning). Filo will come up sides of pan and hang over edges. (Place it evenly so you have the same amount of overhang on each side of pan). Gently butter the overhang, too. Repeat with 6 more layers.

Spoon filling onto buttered filo and spread evenly. Fold edges of filo over top of filling to lay flat. Cut remaining 3 sheets of filo in half. Place on top of spinach mixture, buttering as before, and repeat until filo is gone. Spread any remaining butter on top. Score top into 8 squares if making entree-sized portions, or 32 triangles if serving as appetizers.

Bake, covered with foil, for 50 minutes, or until spanakopita is bubbling; remove foil and bake for 25 minutes more, until top is nicely browned. Allow to cool slightly before serving. While still quite warm, cut through where pieces were scored. Serve warm or at room temperature.

MAKES 6 TO 8 MAIN-DISH OR 16 APPETIZER SERVINGS

Satisfying, healthy, and green—if you like broccoli, you will love this stir-fry. Mushrooms, sesame oil, and tamari add rich flavor. Tofu makes it a main dish. Just add some Confetti Rice (page 83) for a complete meal.

Stir-Fried Broccoli with Mushrooms, Red Onion, and Seasoned Tofu

1 large bunch broccoli (about 1 1/2 pounds)

3 tablespoons olive oil, divided

1 small red onion, sliced in thin half circles (about 1 cup)

8 ounces mushrooms, thinly sliced (use shiitake, cremini, regular large mushrooms, or a combination)

2 tablespoons tamari soy sauce

1 tablespoon water

8 ounces seasoned firm tofu* or 1/2 recipe Marinated Tofu (page 139), cut into 1/4-by-3-inch sticks or 1-by-1 1/2-inch rectangles

2 to 3 teaspoons toasted sesame oil

A few splashes of ume plum vinegar** (optional)

Wash broccoli and remove tough stems. Cut off broccoli florets, dividing them into bite-sized pieces, and cut remaining stem pieces into thin slices about 1/4 by 3 inches. Set aside, keeping stems and florets separate.

In a 12-inch sauté pan, heat 2 tablespoons of the olive oil over medium-high heat. Oil should be quite hot, but not smoking. Add onion and sauté, stirring often, until onion is a little tender, about 5 minutes. Add mushrooms and continue cooking, stirring often, until mushrooms release their liquid and begin to brown, about 8 minutes. Push onions and mushrooms to the edges of pan.

*Seasoned tofu is available at natural food stores. It has been flavored with a marinade and has usually been pressed until firmer than regular tofu.
**Ume plum vinegar is a dark pink Japanese vinegar made from salted *umeboshi* plums. It's available at natural food and Asian markets.

Add remaining tablespoon olive oil to the middle of the pan, and let it get hot. Add broccoli stems and cook, stirring, for about 2 minutes. Add broccoli florets and stir-fry another 2 minutes, browning florets slightly. Add tamari and 1 tablespoon water. Cover and steam, lifting the lid to stir all together occasionally, for 5 to 8 minutes over medium heat, or until broccoli florets are *just* tender (al dente). Add tofu. Remove from heat. Add sesame oil and toss gently; adjust seasonings. If a more piquant flavor is desired, sprinkle on a little ume plum vinegar, to taste. Serve immediately.

MAKES 4 SERVINGS

tuffed Potatoes make a great quick supper, when time and simplicity are of the essence.

Adding plain yogurt instead of sour cream increases the protein (and lowers the fat) substantially or you could make our Ranch-Style Dressing (page 71) to garnish your potato or consider purchasing some of Follow Your Heart's Ranch Dressing—available in the refrigerator section of natural food stores.

Stuffed Potatoes

Four 10-ounce Idaho potatoes (russets)

4 to 8 tablespoons butter or non-hydrogenated margarine

1 recipe Mushroom-Garlic Sauce (page 74) or 12 ounces broccoli, lightly steamed

1 to 2 ounces grated cheddar cheese

Sour cream or yogurt (optional)

1/4 cup chopped green onions

 Preheat oven to 375°F. Wash and pierce potatoes in several places, and bake until tender, about 1 hour.

Make a lengthwise slit in potatoes, opening them a bit, and slip in 1 to 2 tablespoons butter per potato and the Mushroom-Garlic Sauce or broccoli. Top with grated cheese. Return potatoes to the oven for a few minutes, just until cheese melts. Serve immediately, topped with sour cream, if desired, and a sprinkling of green onions.

variation For a vegan version, simply serve the baked potato with a little non-hydrogenated margarine and the Mushroom-Garlic Sauce, broccoli optional. No need to bake the second time.

MAKES 4 SERVINGS

Seasoned tofus can be purchased at natural food stores in several varieties. They are usually very firm and full of flavor, because they're marinated for a long time, then pressed to remove liquid.

I love making my own. Ours is marinated for several hours, and the plain tofu really absorbs flavor. We use very firm tofu to make this, and baking it makes it even firmer.

This homemade teriyaki version has the intense full flavor of wheat-free tamari (most soy sauces are made with wheat, but a few are all soy, and useful for those with wheat allergies). Bragg's Liquid Aminos is another soy-based seasoning with its own distinctive character.

Marinated Tofu would be delicious in Stir-Fried Broccoli with Mushrooms, Red Onion, and Seasoned Tofu (page 136); it would make a great meal served with Confetti Rice (page 83) and Cabbage with Garlic (page 75); or add half of a recipe to the Szechuan Noodle Salad (page 66).

Marinated Tofu

¹/₂ cup sodium-reduced wheat-free tamari or Bragg's Liquid Aminos

¹/₄ cup olive, safflower, or canola oil

1¹/₂ tablespoons maple syrup

1 large clove garlic, pressed or minced

1¹/₂ teaspoons grated peeled fresh ginger

20 ounces firm or extra-firm plain tofu

Whisk together the tamari, oil, maple syrup, garlic, and ginger. Slice tofu into 8 large pieces, about 3 by 3 inches, and marinate in the refrigerator for at least 2 hours, preferably 4 hours or overnight.

Preheat oven to 350°F. Place tofu and marinade on a baking sheet or in a shallow baking dish, and roast it for 25 to 30 minutes, or until nicely browned and most of the marinade has evaporated. Serve warm, or chill, slice, and add to salads.

MAKES 6 TO 8 SERVINGS

A dapted from the *Silver Palate Cookbook*, this Spanish recipe infuses the tofu with a marvelous combination of ingredients. Marinating the tofu overnight is essential to achieve a deep, sweet flavor. Serve over fluffy rice, with all the pan juices.

Tofu Marbella

$^3/_4$ cup pitted prunes

$^1/_2$ cup pitted Spanish green olives

$^1/_2$ head garlic, peeled and finely minced or pressed

$^1/_4$ cup red wine vinegar

$^1/_4$ cup extra-virgin olive oil

$^1/_4$ cup capers with a little juice

2 tablespoons dried oregano

3 bay leaves

Sea salt

Freshly ground black pepper

2 pounds firm tofu, cut into large cubes

$^1/_2$ cup packed brown sugar or Sucanat

$^1/_2$ cup white wine

2 tablespoons finely chopped fresh Italian parsley or cilantro

In a large bowl, combine prunes, olives, garlic, vinegar, oil, capers and juice, oregano, bay leaves, and salt and pepper to taste. Gently fold in the tofu and make sure it is well coated with the marinade. Cover and marinate, in refrigerator overnight or for at least 6 hours.

Preheat oven to 350°F.

Arrange tofu in a single layer in 2 large, shallow baking pans; spoon marinade over it evenly. Sprinkle tofu pieces with sugar and pour wine around them.

Bake for 40 to 50 minutes, basting occasionally with pan juices. Tofu should be nicely browned and flavorful.

With a slotted spoon, transfer tofu, prunes, olives, and capers to a serving platter. Moisten with a few spoonfuls of pan juices; sprinkle generously with parsley.

MAKES 6 SERVINGS

A timbale is a kind of casserole, sometimes layered, and baked in a round dish. Timbale literally means "drum." In this case our timbale is a vegetable casserole made with tofu, with a softer texture than our Wheatloaf (page 143), its close cousin. Baked in a 1-quart soufflé dish, its round shape is very appealing.

Sautéing the vegetables adds great flavor, as does the addition of cumin. Serve with our Simple Tomato Sauce (page 129).

Tofu Timbale

2 tablespoons olive oil + plus extra for greasing dish

2/3 cup chopped onion

1/2 cup finely chopped celery

1/2 cup chopped walnuts

1/2 cup chopped green onions

1 large clove garlic, minced or pressed

1 pound firm tofu, finely crumbled

1 cup quick oats

1/2 cup vegetable broth*

1/3 cup ketchup

1/4 cup finely chopped fresh parsley

1 tablespoon Ener-G Egg Replacer powder

1 tablespoon tamari soy sauce

1 teaspoon Spike seasoning

1 teaspoon ground cumin

1/4 teaspoon sea salt

1/4 teaspoon freshly ground black pepper

Preheat oven to 350°F.

Pour the oil into a large skillet over medium heat. When hot but not smoking, add the onion and celery; sauté about 5 minutes, stirring occasionally, until

*For vegetable broth, you may use one of the many canned, boxed, or frozen products on the market. Or use our Mushroom Stock (page 107). Don't use bouillon!

onion is translucent. Add the walnuts, green onions, and garlic, and sauté another few minutes, stirring often, until nuts and garlic are golden and fragrant. Set aside to cool.

Mix together thoroughly in a large bowl the tofu, oats, broth, ketchup, parsley, egg replacer powder, tamari, Spike, cumin, salt, and pepper. Add cooled veggie mixture. Oil a 1-quart ceramic soufflé dish, and spoon in the timbale mixture, spreading to make a smooth top. Bake, uncovered, for 50 to 60 minutes, or until timbale is golden brown and toothpick inserted in center comes out clean.

Let timbale rest for about 20 minutes. Carefully run a knife or thin spatula around edge of dish to loosen it; turn out onto a serving plate.

MAKES 6 TO 8 SERVINGS

Vegetarian comfort food, this is delicious as a hot main dish with mashed potatoes and Mark's Scrumptious Mushroom Gravy (page 177). It's also wonderful the next day, sliced, for sandwiches. It can be mixed speedily in a food processor or the old-fashioned way, by hand.

wheatloaf

$1/2$ cup bulghur wheat

1 cup water

10 ounces firm tofu, cut into large cubes

$1/3$ cup ketchup, preferably fruit sweetened

$1/4$ cup vegetable broth or Mushroom Stock (page 107)

$1/4$ cup finely chopped fresh parsley

2 tablespoons unsalted butter or non-hydrogenated margarine, softened and cut into small pieces

2 tablespoons tamari soy sauce

1 tablespoon Dijon mustard

$1 1/2$ teaspoons Ener-G Egg Replacer powder

1 large clove garlic, minced or pressed

1 teaspoon Spike seasoning

$1/4$ teaspoon freshly ground black pepper

$2/3$ cup rolled oats

$2/3$ cup finely chopped onion

$1/2$ cup chopped walnuts

$1/4$ cup finely chopped celery

$1/4$ cup chopped green onion

Vegetable oil for greasing pan

Preheat oven to 350°F.

In a small saucepan, bring to a boil the bulghur and water. Turn heat to low, cover, and simmer 15 to 20 minutes, or until water is completely absorbed and bulghur is tender. Let cool to room temperature. Set aside.

Food processor method

In a food processor fitted with the steel blade, combine the tofu, ketchup, broth, parsley, butter, tamari, mustard, egg replacer powder, garlic, Spike, and pepper. Process until smooth, about 5 seconds.

If you've got a large food processor, you can add the cooled, cooked bulghur, oats, onion, walnuts, celery, and green onion, and pulse a few times just to mix (don't process until smooth—this needs to stay a little chunky for texture). If your food processor won't fit all these things, just pour the ketchup mixture into a large bowl and stir in the rest of the ingredients. Mixture will be thick and sticky. Proceed to baking instructions.

Hand method (you will require a blender for blending tofu)

In a large bowl, cream the butter. Add ketchup, parsley, tamari, mustard, egg replacer powder, garlic, Spike, and pepper and stir until thoroughly combined.

Place tofu in a blender with the broth and blend until smooth. Pour this into the ketchup mixture and mix well.

Stir in the cooled bulghur, oats, onion, walnuts, celery, and green onion, and mix well. Mixture will be thick and sticky. Proceed to baking instructions.

Baking

Spoon mixture into well-oiled 9-by-5-inch loaf pan and bake, uncovered, on middle rack of oven for 45 to 50 minutes, or until lightly browned and a toothpick inserted in center comes out clean. Cool 15 to 20 minutes before inverting and slicing.

MAKES 8 SERVINGS

Desserts

Grandma and Grandpa Cook lived on Vancouver Island, in British Columbia. When we visited in August we went berry picking. We picked blueberries and red huckleberries, which grew wild at the foot of a glacier. We brought the berries home, and washed and picked them over while Grandma made pie dough.

Coming from our home in the suburbs of Los Angeles to the island was like visiting another time. She had this great kitchen. A painted sideboard held cooking and baking supplies. A wide single sink had a window overlooking the garden. A door off the kitchen led downstairs to the basement, where shelves of preserves stood in neat, colorful rows.

It was not all idyllic. The summer I was 12, I was determined to learn to make a pie crust. I watched Grandma and tried to imitate her. It was hard for her to let me help. She liked doing things herself and was short on patience. Back in Los Angeles, my next attempt at pie dough was a dismal failure, resulting in the purchase of a store-bought crust.

Shortly thereafter I found a recipe that explained pie dough thoroughly, and I got the hang of it. Use cold butter and ice water. Don't over handle the dough.

I considered it a great accomplishment when I learned to make good pie pastry, so that I could create this simple and wonderful thing: a container to house the sublime (fresh fruit). This pie is a lot like Grandma used to make, minus the Crisco and white sugar. She might not consider their loss an improvement! Just the same, I wish she were still around to taste it.

Blueberry Pie, Revisited

PIE CRUST
$2^1/2$ cups unbleached all-purpose flour + extra for rolling

$1/2$ teaspoon sea salt

12 tablespoons ($1^1/2$ sticks) cold unsalted butter, diced

6 to 7 tablespoons ice water

5 cups fresh blueberries (two 1-pint baskets)

$1/2$ to $3/4$ cup Fruit Source* or unbleached cane sugar

3 tablespoons unbleached all-purpose flour

$1/4$ teaspoon sea salt

$1^1/2$ tablespoons freshly squeezed lemon juice

1 tablespoon cold unsalted butter, diced

Mix flour and salt in a large bowl. With a pastry blender or 2 knives, cut in the butter, until the mixture resembles tiny peas. Sprinkle water over the flour mixture a little at a time, and mix lightly with a fork, using only enough water so that the pastry holds together when pressed into a ball. Handle carefully— don't worry about getting every little scrap of dough into the ball, or it might get tough.

Flatten the dough into a 7-inch disk, then wrap in plastic wrap and chill for 1 hour.

Preheat oven to 425°F. Have ready a 9-inch deep-dish pie pan. Divide the dough into 2 balls. Between sheets of waxed paper, sprinkled with flour, roll out half the dough, to 2 inches larger than the pan. Ease it into the pan, fitting it loosely but firmly. Roll out the top crust and set aside while you prepare filling.

Wash and pick over the blueberries. Mix the Fruit Source, flour, and salt in a large bowl. Add the blueberries and lemon juice and toss well. Pile the mixture into the lined pie pan and dot with butter. Drape the top crust over the pie, and crimp or flute the edges. Cut several vents in the top. Bake for 10 minutes, then lower the heat to 350°F and bake for 30 to 40 minutes, or until the top is browned. Let cool for about an hour before serving, so juice can set up.

MAKES ONE 9-INCH DEEP-DISH PIE, OR 6 TO 8 SERVINGS

*Fruit Source is an ingenious product made from grape juice concentrate and rice dextrin or rice sugar. It looks a lot like brown sugar, but is absorbed more slowly by the body than other sweeteners. You can purchase it at most natural food stores.

Pudding is comfort food. Tuck into your favorite armchair with a parfait glass of pudding and a silver spoon.

Coconut milk is great in combination with tapioca, and its rich flavor is very satisfying—you won't miss the cow's milk. Fresh corn blended into the pudding adds gentle sweetness, and gives it the familiar pale gold color usually produced by egg yolks.

The fresh strawberry topping is thickened with agar-agar, a clear seaweed traditionally used in Japanese cooking, that can be made into a vegetarian Jell-O. We've used just enough agar-agar here to help the topping set when chilled. I know it sounds a bit unusual, but give it a try—it makes a lovely, creamy pudding.

Coconut Tapioca Pudding

$1/2$ cup pearl (small) tapioca

$1^1/4$ cups water, divided

1 cup fresh or frozen corn kernels

$2^1/2$ cups canned coconut milk*

$1/2$ cup mild honey

$1/4$ teaspoon sea salt

1 tablespoon Ener-G Egg Replacer powder

1 tablespoon water

$1/2$ teaspoon vanilla extract

TOPPING

$3/4$ cup coconut milk

$1^1/2$ tablespoons honey

Dash of sea salt

1 tablespoon arrowroot powder

1 tablespoon water

*Canned coconut milk is made by blending the coconut meat with water, and is normally high in fat; check the fat content on the label, though, because it can vary quite a bit, from about 3 to 13 percent fat per can! Reduced-fat coconut milk is readily available and works well in this recipe, but expect the flavor to be less rich. I like to use a coconut milk with at least a 5 to 8 percent fat for this pudding. Also, look for a brand of canned coconut milk that is free of preservatives. (This is not the same thing as the juice present inside a coconut.)

2 teaspoons agar-agar flakes (see Glossary, page 187)

2/3 cup fresh strawberries, halved (quartered if large)

3 large whole strawberries, leaves intact, as garnish

Soak tapioca in 1 cup of the water for 45 minutes. Drain, discard water, and set aside.

Steam or simmer the corn for 3 to 5 minutes, just until tender. drain and set aside.

In a heavy saucepan, place the coconut milk, drained tapioca, honey, and salt. Bring to a boil, stirring often; reduce heat to medium-low and cook, uncovered, for about 25 minutes, stirring often, until tapioca is mostly translucent and mixture is quite thick.

Whisk together the egg replacer powder and 1 tablespoon water until foamy. Whisk into the hot pudding. Remove 1 cup of the pudding and place in a heat-proof blender container along with the drained corn. Cover and blend on low speed until smooth. Add back to pudding, and cook the whole mixture over low heat for 5 minutes more, stirring often, until thick and foamy. Turn off heat and add vanilla. Pour pudding into six 4-ounce custard cups or parfait glasses and refrigerate.

To make topping: Combine coconut milk, honey, and salt. Bring to a boil, then reduce heat to a simmer. Stir together the arrowroot, water, and agar-agar flakes. Whisk into the hot coconut milk mixture, and continue simmering, stirring often, for about 5 minutes. Remove from heat. When cooled slightly, place in a blender container with the sliced strawberries, and blend until smooth. Set aside at room temperature.

When the pudding has cooled and is nearly set, pour a little topping over each cup. Slice the whole strawberries in half lengthwise, retaining leaves and stem, and garnish puddings with half a strawberry each. Chill until very firm, about 2 hours, or you can eat it softer if you can't wait. After they are firm, you can cover with plastic wrap and puddings will keep, covered, in the refrigerator up to 2 days. If you are making it that far ahead, wait to garnish with fresh strawberries just before serving.

MAKES 6 SERVINGS

I consider this cake a breakthrough in natural foods desserts for several reasons. The cake (excluding the glaze) is sweetened with date sugar and maple syrup, both fairly unrefined products, and it doesn't taste too sweet—just very chocolatey. Cocoa is the chocolate used in the cake, which is naturally lower in fat than prepared chocolate. The fat used is either canola oil or high-oleic safflower oil, which are composed primarily of healthy monounsaturated fats. And this recipe is vegan!

The glaze, while rich in cocoa butter, is free of butter or cream, and it constitutes a rather thin coating on the cake. You could also forego the glaze and serve the cake with a simple raspberry sauce (recipe follows).

Chocolate Glaze Cake

2 cups unbleached all-purpose flour

1 cup date sugar

$1/3$ cup baking cocoa, preferably Hershey's, + extra to dust pan

2 teaspoons baking soda

$3/4$ teaspoon sea salt

$1 2/3$ cups cold water

$1/3$ cup maple syrup

$1/3$ cup + 1 tablespoon canola or safflower oil + extra for greasing pan

4 teaspoons apple cider vinegar

2 teaspoons vanilla extract

GLAZE

4 ounces malt-sweetened dairy-free chocolate chips (such as Sunspire brand), available at natural food stores

3 scant tablespoons freshly brewed strong coffee

Preheat oven to 350°F. Prepare a 9-inch springform pan: Grease bottom and sides of pan, line bottom with parchment, grease parchment, then dust pan and parchment with cocoa. Set aside.

In a large bowl, stir together well the flour, sugar, cocoa, baking soda, and salt. In a separate bowl, whisk together the water, maple syrup, oil, vinegar, and vanilla until well combined. Whisk liquid into dry ingredients just until combined; do not overmix. Pour batter into prepared pan, and bake for 40 to 45 minutes on middle rack of oven, until a slightly moist crumb clings to toothpick inserted in the center. Cool in pan 10 minutes on wire rack; unmold and let cool completely on rack.

While cake is cooling, prepare glaze: In a double boiler set over simmering water, combine chocolate chips and coffee. Stir until chocolate is melted and mixture is smooth and glossy. Remove from heat. Let stand until a spreadable consistency, about 20 minutes. When cake is cool but glaze is still a little warm, spread glaze evenly over top and sides of cake, using an angled icing spatula. Serve at room temperature with Raspberry Sauce, if desired.

note This cake should not be refrigerated, as refrigeration dulls the shiny glaze and spoils the fine texture of the cake. It will keep for a couple of days, covered, in a cool spot.

MAKES 8 TO 12 SERVINGS

Raspberry Sauce

One 12-ounce package frozen raspberries, thawed, or 2 cups fresh raspberries

$1/3$ cup mild honey or unbleached cane sugar

$1 1/2$ tablespoons Grand Marnier

Press the berries through a fine sieve. Add the honey and stir until completely dissolved. Add the liqueur and chill until ready to use.

MAKES ABOUT $1 1/2$ CUPS

I love the deep, dark flavor of cakes made with cocoa. This is a moist, tender, and chocolatey snacking cake, particularly great for those of you avoiding fats, but delicious for the rest of us, too. It doesn't need any frosting.

Fat-free Chocolate Cake

3 cups unbleached all-purpose flour

1 cup date sugar

$1/2$ cup cocoa

1 tablespoon baking soda

1 teaspoon sea salt

2 cups water

$2/3$ cup prune baby food (two $2^1/2$-ounce jars)

$1/2$ cup maple syrup

2 tablespoons apple cider vinegar

1 tablespoon vanilla extract

Vegetable oil for greasing pan

Preheat oven to 350°F.

In large bowl, combine flour, sugar, cocoa, baking soda, and salt. Set aside. Whisk together water, prune puree, maple syrup, vinegar, and vanilla. Add dry ingredients and stir just to mix. Pour into greased 9-by-13-inch pan, and bake for 35 to 40 minutes, until toothpick inserted in center comes out clean. Cool completely before cutting into 3-by-3-inch squares.

MAKES 12 SERVINGS

This recipe comes from the old Golden Temple restaurant in Los Angeles. Located near the Farmer's Market at Third and Fairfax, it was run by the group of American Sikhs called 3HO (Healthy, Happy, Holy Organization). The staff dressed all in white, everyone wore turbans, and swords hung from their waists in the traditional Sikh manner. It was always an interesting place to eat, and the food was good—the menu was vegetarian with an emphasis on Indian cuisine. This cake is golden brown, finely textured, moist, and surprisingly light for a cake made with whole wheat flour and without eggs. The chemical reaction of sour cream and baking soda is what makes the cake rise, so make sure your baking soda is very fresh.

Lemon Sesame Cake

11 tablespoons unsalted butter, softened slightly + extra for greasing pan

1 1/4 cups + 2 tablespoons mild honey

1 1/2 teaspoons vanilla extract

1 1/2 tablespoons grated lemon zest

1 1/2 teaspoons lemon extract

3 cups whole wheat pastry flour + extra for pans

1/2 teaspoon sea salt

1/2 cup hulled sesame seeds

1 cup sour cream

1 cup water

1 tablespoon baking soda

1 recipe Luscious Lemon Filling (page 155)

1 recipe Buttercream Frosting (page 156)

Preheat oven to 325°F.

Using an electric mixer, cream together butter, honey, and vanilla until light and fluffy. Add lemon zest and lemon extract and blend well.

In a separate bowl, sift together flour and salt. Stir in sesame seeds. Add flour mixture and sour cream alternately to butter mixture, beginning and ending with dry ingredients. Mix after each addition only enough to combine.

In a small saucepan, bring water to a boil. Remove from heat and stir in baking soda until dissolved. Lightly mix soda mixture into batter, a little at a time. Do not overmix. Let batter sit for 15 minutes.

While batter is resting, prepare two 9-inch round cake pans. Butter pans, then place rounds of parchment or wax paper in bottom; butter parchment, then lightly flour pans. Pour batter into pans and bake for 35 to 40 minutes, or until a toothpick inserted in center comes out clean. Let cakes cool in pans set on a wire rack.

After cakes are cooled, carefully turn 1 layer out onto the plate the cake will be served on. Remove parchment. Spoon Lemon Filling onto top of layer and spread evenly. Turn out second layer on top of this. Frost top and sides with Buttercream Frosting. Serve at room temperature. Cake may be refrigerated, but should be allowed to return to room temperature before serving.

MAKES 12 SERVINGS

Have you ever had lemon curd? It's a British concoction, and is eaten in Canada, too. Traditionally it's made with egg yolks, lemon juice, and sugar. As kids, we liked to spread it on graham crackers and eat it for tea-time, snacks, or dessert.

Our recipe is a lot like lemon curd, though new and improved. It's a tart, lemony spread, designed to use as a layer-cake filling in the Lemon Sesame Cake (page 153). It is not too sweet, with rich, creamy lemon flavor.

Luscious Lemon Filling

4 tablespoons (^{1}/2 stick) unsalted butter

^{1}/4 cup brown rice flour

2 tablespoons kudzu* powder, crushed to remove lumps if necessary, or arrowroot powder

^{3}/4 cup freshly squeezed lemon juice

1 cup honey

1^1/2 teaspoon grated lemon zest

Melt butter. Add flour and stir over low heat 2 minutes (mixture should be bubbling slightly). Remove from heat.

Stir kudzu into the lemon juice until dissolved thoroughly. Add honey and kudzu-lemon juice mixture to butter-flour mixture.

Place over medium heat, and stir often, until mixture is bubbly and thick (2 to 3 minutes). Remove from heat; stir in lemon zest and allow to cool.

This will thicken as it cools; wait to spread on cake layers until after it thickens.

MAKES 1^2/3 CUPS, OR ENOUGH TO COVER TWO 9-INCH LAYERS

*Kudzu or kuzu, a natural thickener similar to arrowroot, is available at most natural food stores.

Now, I like cake. But I love frosting.

Childhood frosting at my house was butter whipped with powdered sugar, vanilla, and sometimes food coloring. My sisters and I loved to bake cakes in our heart-shaped pans. They were usually Duncan Hines, our favorite brand (we rarely made scratch). One of the benefits of cake making was leftover frosting, spread generously on graham crackers.

All of which brings me to this recipe. It is amazingly light. It has a better consistency than the frostings we used to make; it's more like those fluffy frostings the bakeries use, but is made with real butter, not hydrogenated shortening, so it tastes superb. The non-instant milk powder gives it a sweet taste and contributes to its fluffy texture. (Don't use instant milk powder; it won't work. You can purchase the non-instant kind at natural food stores.) It can be prepared up to a couple of days ahead, and stored, tightly covered, in the refrigerator. (Let soften to room temperature before using.) A real treat, and great on our Lemon Sesame Cake (page 153).

Buttercream Frosting

16 tablespoons (2 sticks) unsalted butter, softened

$1/2$ to 1 cup mild honey,* preferably a thick consistency, such as creamed honey

$1/4$ cup safflower or almond oil

$1 1/2$ teaspoons vanilla extract

$3/4$ cup non-instant dry milk powder, sifted (must be very fresh)

Using an electric mixer, beat together the butter, honey, oil, and vanilla until light, white, and fluffy. Add milk powder and beat for about 1 minute more. (An electric mixer, either on a stand or handheld, is essential for making this recipe properly.) Store in refrigerator; let soften to room temperature before using.

MAKES ABOUT 1³/₄ CUPS, OR ENOUGH TO FROST TWO 9-INCH LAYERS

*I prefer this frosting with the smaller amount of honey ($1/2$ cup), but if a sweeter frosting is desired, you may add more with excellent results.

I love these simple cookies and make them every year for Christmas. The powdered sugar melts as it touches the warm cookie, forming a lovely glaze.

Maple Pecan Puffs

8 tablespoons (1 stick) unsalted butter, at room temperature + extra for greasing pans

2 tablespoons maple sugar

1 teaspoon vanilla extract

1 cup shelled pecans, very fresh

1 cup sifted whole wheat pastry flour or spelt flour

$^1/_4$ cup powdered maple sugar (see note below) or organic powdered cane sugar

Preheat oven to 300°F.

With a wooden spoon or an electric mixer, beat butter until soft. Add maple sugar and blend until creamy. Stir in vanilla, and set aside.

Grind pecans in a nut grinder or very briefly in a food processor until a fine meal is formed (if using food processor, just pulse a few seconds, or you will get nut butter).

Stir the ground pecans and flour into the butter mixture. Roll dough into small balls, about 1$^1/_4$ inches in diameter. Place balls on greased cookie sheets about $^3/_4$ inch apart. Bake on upper rack of oven for about 20 minutes, until cookies have a nice roasted smell and bottoms are just lightly browned (check periodically to make sure bottoms are not browning too quickly—if so, reduce heat to 275°F and continue). While still hot, roll cookies in powdered sugar. After cooling, store in an airtight container.

I imagine they'd keep for about a week, but they never last that long!

MAKES ABOUT FORTY 1$^1/_2$-INCH BALLS

note To make powdered maple sugar, place about $^1/_4$ cup maple sugar in an electric coffee grinder, spice grinder, or the small (1 cup) attachment of a blender. Grind at high speed for about 20 seconds, or until sugar is very fine and powdery (it won't be as fine as regular powdered sugar).

Extremely refreshing. I can't imagine a nicer dessert on a warm summer evening, following a meal of simple pasta and a crisp salad.

Often when I make this, I combine watermelon and cantaloupe. It's a gorgeous peachy color and the flavor is spectacular.

Melon Sorbet

5 cups seeded and cubed melon (approximately 2 medium cantaloupes, but feel free to use watermelon, honeydew, or whatever you like)

3 tablespoons mild honey (like clover) or unbleached cane sugar

2 tablespoons freshly squeezed lemon juice

Combine all ingredients in bowl of food processor and puree. Chill mixture until it is quite cold to the touch, about 1 hour, then freeze in ice cream maker according to manufacturer's directions.

MAKES 1 QUART, OR 4 TO 6 SERVINGS

Most sorbets are way too sweet. That's the beauty of making your own. Choose gorgeous berries at the peak of ripeness and you'll need little added sweetener. Serve a ravishing red scoop of this with honeydew Melon Sorbet (above).

Strawberry Sorbet

5 cups whole strawberries (approximately two 1-pint baskets)

1 cup raspberry juice (I use an organic frozen concentrate, diluted with water as directed, because it has a strong raspberry flavor. It's available at natural food stores. If not available, use a bottled raspberry apple juice with no sugar added.)

2 tablespoons freshly squeezed lemon juice

1/4 cup mild honey or unbleached cane sugar (adjust amount to taste)

Combine all ingredients in blender or food processor and puree until smooth. Chill mixture for about an hour, or until cold to the touch, then freeze in ice cream maker according to manufacturer's directions.

MAKES ABOUT 1 QUART, OR 4 TO 6 SERVINGS

Finely ground nuts add a richness and depth of flavor quite beyond a regular flour crust. This makes a fine pastry for our Happy Chicken Pot Pie (page 114).

Also a great foil for certain fruit pies, such as peach or apple; as a single crust, try it as a base for a fresh strawberry or plum tart.

Nutty Pie Crust

$1/2$ cup walnut halves or large pieces

$1/2$ cup almonds (skin left on)

$1 1/2$ cups unbleached all-purpose flour

1 cup whole wheat pastry flour

8 tablespoons (1 stick) unsalted butter or non-hydrogenated margarine, cold

$1/2$ teaspoon sea salt

1 cup + 2 tablespoons ice water

In the bowl of a food processor fitted with the steel blade and large enough to hold all ingredients, place the walnuts and almonds. Process to a fine meal, about 30 seconds; watch carefully so as not to make nut butter. Turn off processor and add flours, butter, and salt. Pulse on and off quickly for about 15 seconds, until mixture resembles a coarse meal. With machine running, pour water through feed tube; keep running until mixture forms a ball, 5 to 10 seconds. Turn off machine. Wrap in plastic and chill for 1 hour before rolling out.

For rolling, see instructions for Happy Chicken Pot Pie (page 114). To bake, follow directions for the particular fruit or savory pie you are making. It bakes at about the same temperature and in the same amount of time as a regular flour crust.

MAKES ONE DOUBLE CRUST FOR 9-INCH REGULAR OR DEEP-DISH PIE

Basic pie crust—this is an essential recipe: Once mastered, it will be used again and again for both sweet and savory applications. It is tender, flaky, and golden, owing much to the generous quantity of butter. You can make pie pastry with less fat, and it will taste good. But this one tastes great, has superb texture, and is easy to handle. Why mess around? How often do you make pie?

I love the mix of whole wheat pastry flour with unbleached white. Flavorful, but still delicate. Of course, you could use all white or all whole wheat, but expect the flavor and texture to vary.

I've also substituted other flours successfully: spelt, both white and whole grain; barley flour; and brown rice flour. Feel free to experiment, especially if you are cooking for someone who is allergic to wheat. Alternative grains have their own unique flavors. Because it is more sticky, pastry made from barley and rice is more difficult to handle, and will need to be rolled out between sheets of waxed paper or plastic wrap.

Pastry Crust (Butter) for Pie

1 $1/2$ cups unbleached all-purpose flour

1 cup whole wheat pastry flour

1 teaspoon maple sugar, Sucanat, or unbleached cane sugar (optional)

$1/2$ teaspoon sea salt

16 tablespoons (2 sticks) unsalted butter, very cold and cubed

$1/4$ to $1/2$ cup ice water

If mixing dough by hand

In a large bowl, combine flours, sugar, and salt; mix well. Add butter to flour mixture and cut in with a pastry cutter or 2 knives, until mixture looks like coarse cornmeal. Add $1/4$ cup water, stirring mixture quickly with a fork, until a dough is formed—if more water is needed, add a little at a time, continuing to stir, until dough forms. Dough should be soft but not sticky.

Flatten dough into an 8-inch disk, wrap tightly with plastic, and chill for 1 hour. (Follow rolling and baking instructions with individual recipes.)

If using food processor

Place flours, sugar, and salt in bowl of food processor fitted with the steel blade. Process a few seconds, just to combine. Add butter to bowl. Process a few seconds, until mixture looks like coarse cornmeal. With machine running, add $1/4$ cup ice water through the feed tube; if dough doesn't form into a ball, add a little more water until it does. Stop machine as soon as ball forms. Shape, wrap, and chill as above.

MAKES 1 DOUBLE-CRUST 8- TO 10-INCH PIE PASTRY, OR ENOUGH FOR 1 LARGE CROSTATA

I love the look of this dessert: golden mounds of baked biscuit dough covering perfectly ripe, warm fruit. I eagerly await July, when my favorite "Magpie" peaches, juicy and sweet, are available at the farmer's market. It's a classic summer dessert: easy, unpretentious, and delicious. Great with berries, too.

Peach (or Berry) Cobbler

5 cups peeled and sliced ripe peaches (about 5 medium peaches) or 5 cups fresh whole blackberries or sliced strawberries

$^1/_3$ cup mild honey + 2 tablespoons for dough*

1 teaspoon grated lemon zest

1 tablespoon freshly squeezed lemon juice

$^1/_4$ teaspoon almond extract (omit if using berries)

$1^1/_2$ cups unbleached all-purpose flour** + 1 tablespoon to mix with filling

1 tablespoon baking powder

$^1/_2$ teaspoon sea salt

$5^1/_3$ tablespoons ($^2/_3$ stick) unsalted butter or non-hydrogenated margarine, cold and cubed + extra for greasing dish

$1^1/_2$ teaspoons Ener-G Egg Replacer powder

2 tablespoons water

$^1/_4$ cup milk or honey soymilk

Preheat oven to 400°F. Butter a 2-quart baking dish (approximately 8 by 12 inches).

Place fruit in baking dish. Drizzle with $^1/_3$ cup honey, and sprinkle with lemon zest, lemon juice, and almond extract, if using. Sprinkle 1 tablespoon flour evenly over peaches, and toss mixture gently just until flour dissolves. Set aside.

*Maple sugar or unbleached cane sugar can be used in place of the final tablespoon of honey, sprinkled over the top, for a golden brown, sugary crust.
** You can substitute up to $^3/_4$ cup whole wheat pastry flour for an equal amount of white flour, if so desired.

Sift remaining 1¹/₂ cups flour, baking powder, and salt together into a bowl. Cut in butter until mixture resembles cornmeal. Whisk egg replacer powder into water until foamy. Add milk and 1 tablespoon honey, and mix this into dry ingredients until just combined.

Drop dough by large spoonfuls over surface of fruit. Drizzle with remaining tablespoon honey, in a fine stream. Bake for about 20 minutes, or until top is golden brown and fruit is bubbling.

Serve warm, topped with whipped cream or vanilla ice cream, or as is.

MAKES 6 TO 8 SERVINGS

A festival of fresh fruit. The lemon pastry cream is delightfully light, and is made with tofu instead of the usual milk or cream. The crust is flaky and scrumptious, even though it's made with oil. (If you prefer a butter crust, however, you can use the recipe on page 160.)

Use any fresh fruit you enjoy: strawberries, kiwi, tangerines, apricots, or a rainbow combination. Just match the color and flavor of the fruit with a suitable jam—apricot, being light colored, would work for the orange fruits and even on kiwi. If you are using both light and dark fruits, you'll want to use more than one kind of jam.

Mandala Fruit Tart

TART PASTRY

1 cup unbleached all-purpose flour

$^1/_4$ teaspoon sea salt

$^1/_4$ cup safflower oil

2 tablespoons cold soymilk*

PASTRY CREAM

One 10-ounce package Mori-Nu silken, lite, extra-firm tofu

$^1/_4$ cup water + 1 tablespoon for jam

1 package Mori-Nu Lemon Pudding mix (powdered)

$^1/_4$ teaspoon vanilla extract

$^1/_4$ cup strawberry, black currant, apricot, or raspberry jam

1 pint (more or less) fresh strawberries, preferably small and perfectly ripe, or 2 cups of any other beautiful, ripe fruits, singly or in combination: raspberries, blackberries, peeled sliced kiwi, apricot halves, seedless tangerine slices, Fuyu persimmon slices, mango slices, etc.

Fresh mint leaves as garnish

 Preheat oven to 450°F.

---

*I use refrigerated honey soymilk in this crust and in most baking recipes. I prefer its clean, light taste to the soymilk in the aseptic boxes, but if you do use one of the others, make sure it is plain, without added flavorings.

Whisk together flour and salt in a mixing bowl. Combine oil and milk in a measuring cup (do not stir); add, all at once, to flour mixture. Stir lightly with a fork until mixture comes together. Form into a ball and flatten slightly with hands.

Roll ball between sheets of waxed paper to about a 10-inch diameter (dampen work surface with a little water to prevent paper from slipping).

Peel off top paper, and flip dough, paper side up, into a 9-inch tart pan with removable bottom. Remove paper. Press dough snugly into the pan, trimming off any excess crust (there won't be much—this is pretty much a perfect fit), which you can use to fill in any thin spots. Crust should just be level with top of pan, and an even thickness all around sides. Prick dough with a fork in several places to prevent buckling during baking.

Bake 10 to 12 minutes in middle of oven or until a light golden brown. Cool on a wire rack.

To make pastry cream: In a blender container or food processor, blend the tofu and $^1/_4$ cup water until smooth and creamy. If using a blender, you may need to stop and scrape the sides frequently. Once smooth, add the lemon pudding mix and vanilla and continue blending for 2 to 3 minutes, stopping and scraping as necessary, until mixture is very creamy. Set aside.

When tart pastry is cooled, spread about half the pastry cream into the crust, smoothing with a spatula (save the rest of the pastry cream for another tart or eat as pudding). Chill tart shell with pastry cream for about $^1/_2$ hour.

Meanwhile, heat the jam with 1 tablespoon water, and then press through a fine-mesh sieve into a bowl. If using strawberries, gently rinse and carefully dry strawberries, remove stems, and slice in half if small, or in 4 widthwise slices if large. Lay berries across surface of tart in concentric circles or a pattern of your choosing. Brush or spoon sieved jam across surface of berries, avoiding pastry cream. Garnish with mint leaves and serve immediately. (You may chill the tart for an hour or two, tightly wrapped, but the crust will lose its crispness after much longer than that.) If using other fruits, follow the general idea as for the strawberries, slicing fruit attractively and arranging in beautiful patterns. You can overlap fruit. Leave raspberries or blackberries whole.

MAKES 6 SERVINGS

A crostata is a rustic pie, in this case filled with pears. It's easier to make than a double-crust pie: You roll out only one piece of dough into a large circle, place it on a baking sheet or in a pie plate, fill with pears, then fold the sides of the dough up over the fruit. This leaves the center of the crostata open with sliced pears peeking out. It looks dramatic, and like you went to a lot of trouble. Ginger adds elegance, and zip.

Pear Crostata

Flour for rolling pastry

1 recipe Pastry Crust for Pie (page 160), chilled

2 1/2 pounds D'Anjou pears (about 5 large)

1/2 cup + 1 to 2 tablespoons maple sugar or unbleached cane sugar

1 teaspoon ground ginger, divided

1 tablespoon melted butter

Preheat oven to 400°F.

On a floured board, roll pastry 1/8 inch thick, to a diameter with an edge all around of 16 inches. Gently fold in half, and carefully transfer to a large baking sheet with an edge all around, or 10-inch pie plate. Unfold dough—if using pie plate, it will drape over sides.

Peel, halve, and core the pears. Slice lengthwise thickly, about 4 or 5 slices per half, then slice crosswise once more. (Yield: about 8 cups sliced pears.) Spread half the pears in the center of the tart, about 8 inches in diameter, leaving a 4-inch-wide border. Sprinkle pears with 1/4 cup of the maple sugar and 1/2 teaspoon ginger; add rest of pears, 1/4 cup more sugar, and remaining 1/2 teaspoon ginger.

Working in one direction, fold up sides of tart, until the sides are enclosed, leaving an open center of 4 to 6 inches. (The dough will overlap a little at the "corners" that form.) Press firmly but gently to seal dough. (If you're baking the crostata on a baking sheet, you'll want to make sure the dough is well sealed and has no holes or tears, or liquid will leak through.)

Brush dough with butter, and pour any remainder over pears. Sprinkle with the 1 to 2 tablespoons remaining maple sugar. Bake for 15 minutes, then reduce heat to 350°F for 20 to 25 minutes, or until nicely browned.

Serve warm or at room temperature, with ice cream or whipped cream if desired.

MAKES 8 TO 10 SERVINGS

Thin, crisp, flavorful cookies emerge from this rolled cookie dough. They look like gingerbread and are spicy like gingerbread, but the peanut butter is a delightful surprise.

Originally designed for Halloween using bat, witch, and other scary shapes, this recipe was clipped by Thelma Moody, mother of my friend Laurie Dean, from a Detroit newspaper years ago. It's been updated in the style of Follow Your Heart.

Thelma's Halloween Peanut Butter Cookie Crisps

3 cups sifted unbleached all-purpose flour + extra for rolling dough

1 teaspoon ground ginger

1 teaspoon ground cinnamon

$^1/_2$ teaspoon sea salt

$^1/_2$ teaspoon baking powder

$^1/_4$ teaspoon baking soda

$^1/_4$ teaspoon ground cloves

8 tablespoons (1 stick) unsalted butter or non-hydrogenated margarine

$^1/_2$ cup creamy unsalted peanut butter

$^2/_3$ cup Sucanat* or dark brown cane sugar

$1^1/_2$ teaspoons Ener-G Egg Replacer powder

2 tablespoons water

$^1/_2$ cup unsulphured Barbados molasses, or other light molasses (not blackstrap)

 In a large bowl, stir together flour, ginger, cinnamon, salt, baking powder, baking soda, and cloves. Set aside.

In another large bowl, cream butter and peanut butter until smooth; add Sucanat and mix thoroughly. Whisk together the egg replacer powder and water until frothy, and stir this and the molasses into the butter mixture, until all is

*Sucanat is a granular cane sweetener available at natural food stores.

incorporated. Gradually add flour mixture, about one quarter of it at a time, and stir until all is thoroughly mixed. Wrap dough in plastic wrap or wax paper, and chill for 1 hour, or until firm enough to roll.

Preheat oven to 350°F.

Cut dough into 4 parts, working with one quarter at a time, keeping the rest refrigerated.

On a floured board, roll dough as thinly as possible, about $^1/_8$ inch to $^1/_{15}$ inch.

Cut dough into desired shapes and place $^1/_2$ inch apart on ungreased cookie sheets. (This dough is delicate, especially when rolled thin, so smaller shapes work better.) Bake until lightly browned around edges, 6 to 7 minutes. Cool on racks. After cooling, store in airtight containers.

MAKES APPROX. 5 DOZEN COOKIES

This rolled dough makes a crisp and spicy, light brown gingerbread, perfect for gingerbread people, houses, and other shapes.

Sucanat, the main sweetener in this recipe, is made from granulated cane juice, organically grown (see Glossary). It is best used in recipes with bold spices such as this one because of its assertive flavor.

Gingerbread Cookies

2 3/4 cups whole wheat pastry flour + extra for rolling dough

1 tablespoon baking powder

1 1/2 teaspoons ground ginger

1 teaspoon ground cinnamon

1/2 teaspoon sea salt

1/16 teaspoon ground cloves

1/2 cup Sucanat or dark brown cane sugar

1 1/2 teaspoons Ener-G Egg Replacer powder

2 tablespoons water

8 tablespoons (1 stick) unsalted butter or non-hydrogenated margarine, melted + extra for greasing pans

1/2 cup unsulphured Barbados molasses, or other light molasses (not blackstrap)

Preheat oven to 300°F. Sift together flour, baking powder, ginger, cinnamon, salt, and cloves. Stir in Sucanat and mix well. Whisk together egg replacer powder and water until dissolved and slightly foamy. In another large bowl, stir together butter, molasses, and egg replacer. Add flour mixture gradually, stirring just until dry ingredients are absorbed (dough will be slightly sticky). Wrap in plastic wrap and chill for 1 hour, then roll on floured board to a thickness of about 1/8 inch, and cut with cookie cutters. Bake on a greased or parchment-lined baking sheet for 12 to 15 minutes, or until *lightly* browned.

Let sit on pans for 2 minutes, then carefully transfer to cooling racks. The cookies will crisp as they cool. Store in airtight containers.

MAKES 4 DOZEN MEDIUM COOKIES, OR 1 SMALL GINGERBREAD HOUSE

A Holiday Feast

Follow Your Heart's annual Thanksgiving dinner is served on the Tuesday and Wednesday of Thanksgiving week, and it is our biggest restaurant event of the year. Longtime customers and former employees, some of whom live out of town and come back for the holidays, gather for what constitutes a vegetarian reunion.

Follow Your Heart has become much more than a restaurant over the years. Many friendships, marriages, and families have sprouted here. Some recipes are named after the cooks that invented them, such as Mark's Scrumptious Mushroom Gravy (page 177). I always remember Mark Levitsky when I make this; he and his brother Brion, both talented cooks, each had a stint cooking at the restaurant, as did several other sibling combos, including the Sullivan *and* O'Sullivan sisters.

One year I taught a group of cooking students to make the Thanksgiving Happy Turkey (page 179) with Rice and Mushroom Stuffing (page 178). They enjoyed the "veggie" turkey, and were amazed to discover later that their non-vegetarian families loved it as well.

Our holiday menu at the restaurant is a little different every year, as cooks and cooking styles change. Here are some of our favorite recipes.

Cousin Irene attended most of my childhood Thanksgivings. When she kissed me at the door, I noticed the soft skin of her face, and her lovely pastel dress and matching sweater. In her arms was a white enameled kettle filled with her famous cranberry sauce. No one ever asked her to bring anything else. We could count on her for that perfectly cooked sauce, with hints of cinnamon and orange, like rubies on our plates.

Cousin Irene's Cranberry Sauce

$1/2$ cup water

$1/2$ cup mild honey (like clover; not wildflower) or unbleached cane sugar

$1/4$ cup freshly squeezed orange juice

2 cinnamon sticks

One 12-ounce package whole cranberries, fresh or frozen

2 tablespoons grated fresh orange zest

In a saucepan, combine water, honey, juice, and cinnamon. Bring to a boil; add cranberries, reduce heat to simmer, and continue cooking and stirring occasionally, uncovered, 5 to 7 minutes, or until cranberries pop. Add orange zest and simmer 5 minutes more. Serve warm or chilled.

MAKES ABOUT 2 CUPS

The best kind of comfort food: plump, juicy little onions and sweet baby peas. Brown rice flour, used here as a thickener, imparts a slightly nutty flavor.

Creamed Onions and Peas

2 pints fresh white boiling onions (slightly larger than pearl onions)

One 10-ounce package frozen petite peas or 2 cups freshly shelled peas

4 tablespoons ($^1/_2$ stick) unsalted butter

$^1/_4$ cup brown rice flour or unbleached all-purpose flour

2 cups milk

1 bay leaf

Onion powder

Sea salt

Rinse onions; cut off root and stem ends. Place in a large pot with ample water to cover. Bring to a boil; reduce heat and simmer about 5 minutes, or until onions are tender but still intact. Drain immediately and allow to cool. When cool enough to touch, slip off the tough outer skins and discard them, being careful to keep the onions whole. Cover and set aside.

If using frozen peas, rinse under hot water to thaw; drain and set aside before adding to sauce. If using fresh shelled peas, simmer or steam them for just a few minutes, until bright green and slightly tender. Set aside and prepare white sauce.

In a 3-quart saucepan, melt butter over low heat. Add flour and continue cooking, stirring constantly, for 3 to 4 minutes, or until the taste of raw flour has vanished, and mixture gives off a pleasant roasted smell.

Slowly whisk in the milk, $^1/_2$ cup at a time. Add bay leaf, and onion powder and sea salt to taste. Simmer the sauce and continue whisking constantly until it is thickened, smooth, and quite hot. Reduce heat to low; stir in cooked onions and peas. Adjust seasonings to taste. (I like to use a lot of onion powder for a full flavor.) Serve hot. This can be reheated in a double boiler just before serving.

MAKES 8 SERVINGS

Italian in origin, this side dish with its bright flavor and color is a gorgeous addition to the holiday table. Simple, too—make the dressing a day ahead, but cook the broccoli at the very last minute.

Broccoli in Caper Sauce

Sea salt

2 pounds broccoli, cut into florets, stems cut into 1 1/2-inch slices

20 sprigs fresh Italian parsley

4 tablespoons capers

1 clove garlic, pressed

1/2 cup extra-virgin olive oil

Freshly ground black pepper

Set a pot of cold water over high heat and bring to a boil; add salt to taste. Drop broccoli in for 2 to 4 minutes, or until just cooked and still bright green. Drain and transfer to a serving platter.

Finely chop the parsley, capers, and garlic in a food processor. Add oil and blend again. Add salt and pepper to taste.

Pour over broccoli, toss, and serve.

MAKES 6 SERVINGS

Garnet yams, with their orange-red flesh, make a spectacular presentation; they're also naturally sweet. Our glaze is a surprise: refreshingly lemony, still sweet and sticky, but a heap more sophisticated than miniature marshmallows.

Garnet Yams with Maple-Lemon Glaze

8 small garnet yams (about 3 pounds)

4 tablespoons ($^1/_2$ stick) unsalted butter + extra for greasing dish

1 teaspoon arrowroot or kudzu powder (see Glossary, page 187)

2 tablespoons water

$^1/_3$ cup maple syrup

2 tablespoons freshly squeezed lemon juice

1 teaspoon freshly grated lemon zest

Ground cinnamon (optional)

Preheat oven to 400°F. Wash and dry yams and place in a shallow greased baking dish, large enough to hold the yams in a single layer. Bake for 20 minutes; remove yams from oven and pierce* each one once or twice with a sharp knife. (This allows steam to escape and prevents bursting.) Return yams to oven and continue baking 20 to 30 minutes, or until thickest parts are tender.

While yams are baking, prepare maple glaze. Melt butter in a saucepan. Dissolve arrowroot in water. Remove butter from heat and add maple syrup, lemon juice, lemon zest, and arrowroot mixture. Bring to a boil, stirring constantly just until it thickens. Remove from heat.

When yams are tender, remove from oven. Carefully make a long slit lengthwise across top of each yam, and push openings back a little on both sides with a fork. Spoon about 1 tablespoon of the glaze inside each yam. Dust each yam lightly with cinnamon, if desired. Return to oven and bake an additional 10 minutes. Serve.

MAKES 8 SERVINGS

*When piercing yams to prevent bursting and when testing for tenderness, use the point of a sharp knife, and make the puncture along the same lines you will later use to slice open the yams. This will keep them looking good, and not like they were poked and prodded with a dull fork.

Sometimes vegetarians have just got to have some of that rich, meaty flavor. Fabulous over mashed potatoes, stuffing, or Happy Turkey.

Mark's Scrumptious Mushroom Gravy

6 tablespoons (³/4 stick) unsalted butter

3 cups thinly sliced mushrooms (about 8 ounces)

1 tablespoon tamari soy sauce

6 tablespoons brown rice flour or whole wheat pastry flour

2¹/2 cups milk

¹/2 cup half-and-half

1 to 2 tablespoons Bragg's Liquid Aminos

Melt butter in a large skillet on low heat. Add and sauté the mushrooms and tamari. Cook for about 5 minutes, stirring occasionally, until mushrooms are slightly tender.

Slowly add flour. This will become thick and pasty; stir constantly as you continue cooking for 5 minutes, or until mixture has a pleasant roasted smell. Gradually add milk, stirring all the while, then half-and-half. Continue stirring constantly as you bring mixture back to a simmer. When it begins to bubble and thicken, remove from heat. Stir in the Liquid Aminos, and adjust seasonings to taste. Serve hot, over Thanksgiving Happy Turkey and stuffing or mashed potatoes.

MAKES 8 SERVINGS

Perfectly delicious tucked inside our Happy Turkey, and great as a side dish on its own.

For years I've made this with long-grain brown rice, but lately have been experimenting with the wide varieties of whole grain rices available. The four Lundberg brothers in California sell rice from their family farm. In addition to regular brown rice, some of which is organically grown, they sell packages of mixed rice in a rainbow of jewel-like colors and an array of flavors: fat round grains of dark red rice, black Japonica, and brown basmati, to name but a few. I especially like their Wild Blend for this recipe, which contains five different whole grain rices.

Rice and Mushroom Stuffing

4 tablespoons ($^1/_2$ stick) unsalted butter

2 cups finely chopped onion

2 cups diced celery

2 cups thinly sliced mushrooms

$^1/_4$ cup (1 ounce) slivered almonds

$^1/_4$ cup (1 ounce) sunflower seeds or pine nuts

3 cups cooked brown rice (2 cups water to 1 cup raw brown rice), cooled

1 tablespoon dried parsley

$^1/_2$ teaspoon dried thyme

Sea salt or 1 tablespoon tamari soy sauce

Melt butter in a large heavy skillet. Add onion, celery, mushrooms, almonds, and sunflower seeds. Sauté, stirring frequently, until veggies and nuts are golden, a little tender, and onions taste sweet, about 10 minutes. Turn off heat.

Mix the cooked rice with the sautéed veggies and add the parsley, thyme, and salt to taste. (If you use tamari, it will make stuffing a darker color.)

Serve as is, or follow directions for stuffing the Thanksgiving Happy Turkey (page 179).

MAKES 8 SERVINGS

Our Thanksgiving Happy Turkey captures the essence of the season; you don't need to be a vegetarian to enjoy it. Tofu has hit the mainstream.

What is Happy Turkey? It's a vegetarian entree with sass. The holiday flavor takes you back. Its texture is not really like turkey; it's tender and moist, like a vegetarian meatloaf. Sage and thyme lend the distinctive, familiar flavor of poultry seasoning.

It's fun to get carried away with the presentation, shaping this over a mound of stuffing so that it looks like a turkey. Or simply bake it in a loaf pan. Leftover, it slices up into great sandwich fixings. And there's no fighting over the white and dark meat.

Thanksgiving Happy Turkey

3 cups diced yellow onion

1 1/2 cups diced celery

1/4 cup safflower oil

Two 16-ounce packages firm tofu

2 cups (about 9 ounces) raw cashew pieces

2 large cloves garlic, minced or pressed

1 teaspoon celery seed

1/2 teaspoon dried sage

1/2 teaspoon dried thyme

1 1/2 tablespoons arrowroot powder

1/2 cup water

2 to 3 tablespoons tamari soy sauce

Preheat oven to 350°F.

In a medium skillet over medium-high heat, sauté onion and celery in oil until golden and slightly tender.

Crumble tofu into pieces the size of peas and place in a large bowl. In a food processor, grind cashew pieces until fine and powdery (but don't make cashew butter), and add to tofu. Stir in the celery and onion, garlic, celery seed, sage, and thyme.

Dissolve arrowroot in water, then add to tofu mixture. Add tamari to taste.

Place mixture in a 9-by-5-inch loaf pan, and bake for about 1 hour, until nicely browned and firm to the touch.

OR shape the loaf into a turkey shape. Use Rice and Mushroom Stuffing (page 178) or your favorite bread or other stuffing. When stuffing is cool enough to handle, transfer it to a 9-by-13-inch greased baking dish. Shape into a tightly packaged oval mound in center of dish. Pat the Happy Turkey mixture over the stuffing, covering it completely. Shape like a turkey, with legs and all. Bake at 325°F, covered, for 1 hour. Remove cover and bake an additional 20 to 30 minutes, until nicely browned all over. After baking, garnish the "turkey" with bay leaves over the breast in a feather pattern, if desired. Serve, topped with Mark's Scrumptious Mushroom Gravy (page 177) or Mushroom-Garlic Sauce (page 74).

MAKES 8 SERVINGS

Classic pumpkin pie with a twist—no eggs or dairy! Silken tofu and almond butter replace them without sacrificing rich, creamy taste. Your guests may not notice anything is missing, but they'll recognize a delicious pumpkin pie when they taste it.

Pumpkin Pie

2 3/4 cups canned pumpkin (about 25 ounces) or mashed fresh pumpkin puree (see instructions below)

6 tablespoons water

1 tablespoon Ener-G Egg Replacer powder

1 cup brown rice syrup

4 ounces silken firm tofu (such as Mori-Nu brand in the non-refrigerator boxes)

2 1/2 tablespoons almond butter

1 1/2 tablespoons unsulphured Barbados molasses or other light molasses (not blackstrap)

1 tablespoon vanilla extract

1 1/4 teaspoons ground cinnamon

3/4 teaspoon ground allspice

1/2 teaspoon sea salt

2 tablespoon agar-agar flakes (not powdered or bar form; see Glossary, page 187)

1/2 cup soymilk or multigrain beverage

One 9-inch baked single pie crust (use Pastry Crust for Pie page 160)

If not using canned pumpkin, prepare fresh: Don't use the big jack-o-lantern pumpkins, use the small Sugar Pie variety, which tastes much sweeter and has a denser flesh. One pound of whole, uncooked pumpkin equals about 1 1/2 cups, cooked and mashed (so bake 2 pounds of pumpkin for this). Cut open pumpkin and scrape out seeds and pulp. (Save seeds for roasting later.*) Cut into large

*To roast pumpkin seeds: Clean whole seeds thoroughly, rinsing and discarding stringy fibers. Dry seeds on towels. Preheat oven to 300°F. Toss seeds with a little salt or soy sauce, and spread on an ungreased jellyroll pan or baking sheet. Roast for 25 minutes, then take them out and stir seeds to loosen and brown the other sides. Return to oven for 20 to 35 minutes more, or until seeds are crisp. Cool and store in airtight container.

pieces, about 4 by 6 inches, and place skin sides up in a steamer. Steam for about 30 minutes, or until pumpkin tests tender with a fork. Allow to cool. Scrape flesh from skin and discard skin; mash pumpkin thoroughly with a potato masher, or puree in a food processor, until smooth. Set aside and proceed with recipe.

Whisk together water and egg replacer powder until foamy. Place rice syrup, tofu, almond butter, molasses, vanilla, egg replacer mixture, cinnamon, allspice, and salt in blender container and blend until smooth. Set aside.

In a 3-quart saucepan, sprinkle agar-agar flakes into soymilk and let sit 5 minutes. Bring mixture to a boil, and stir to dissolve agar-agar; reduce heat to simmer. Continue stirring for a couple of minutes, or until agar-agar flakes are still visible, but translucent. Add tofu mixture and return mixture to a boil, stirring constantly. Once it boils, continue to stir for 2 minutes. Remove from heat. Stir in pumpkin and mix thoroughly. Pour mixture into baked pie shell and allow to cool. Refrigerate until set, about 4 hours. Slice and serve, with whipped cream if desired.

MAKES 8 TO 10 SERVINGS

Baking Notes

STROLL THROUGH THE FLOUR AISLE of a good natural food store and you'll be amazed at the variety. Flour is the finely ground product of grain; flour is most often made from wheat, and if a recipe calls for one cup of flour, wheat is what's meant. Even so, there are several different kinds of wheat flour. You should be well acquainted with the different varieties. (See Glossary, page 187).

For those who are allergic to wheat or gluten (the protein found in wheat and some other grains) or those who'd like to try other types of flours, there are many alternatives available. They don't behave the same as wheat flour, however, because they contain less or no gluten. It's difficult to find anything that imitates wheat in bread making. Substitute flours work best in cakes, cookies, pie crusts, and pancakes, where the missing gluten factor (which forms the light, strong structure of bread) is not so easily noticed. (See Glossary, Flour and Grain Alternatives, page 188).

Any whole grain flour must be fresh. The germ and bran from the grain is included in whole grain flours, and this is what contains most of the nutrients.

It also contains oil, and this goes rancid rather quickly. Don't eat it if it tastes bitter or stale. Buy from a store that has a rapid turnover of goods, so it's fresh when you purchase it, and don't store whole grain flour for more than four months at room temperature. You can prolong its life by keeping it tightly wrapped in the refrigerator or freezer. Flour will keep for several months this way, depending on how protectively it is wrapped. I have stored flour in glass jars with non-rusting lids, or double bagged in freezer bags.

White flours result in a lighter, whiter product, but they are missing the fiber and nutrients in whole wheat flour. In this book, we use both white and whole grain flours, depending on the recipe and the results we want. If you want to substitute whole grain for white, then make your substitutions by the type of flour used: Substitute whole wheat bread flour for white bread flour, and whole wheat pastry flour for all-purpose flour or cake flour when making cakes, pie crust, muffins, or cookies. Whole grain flour is heavier in baking and usually produces a denser product. However, I often substitute half of the white flour called for in a recipe with whole grain flour. In most recipes, you can get away with this without changing the texture too much, and I prefer the whole grain flavor. Some recipes seem pretty light and fluffy even when using all whole grain flour, like our Potato Focaccia (page 123)—there is enough rising action from the yeast and the potatoes to do the trick. But not all recipes are as forgiving.

Rising

Fresh baking soda and baking powder, as well as a fresh box of egg replacer (which includes rising as well as thickening agents) are vital to eggless baking, because there are no eggs to help leaven the baked goods. I buy small boxes or cans of these as needed, and replace or use them up every few months. Store them in a dry cupboard.

Use a double-acting baking powder such as Rumford's, which is free of aluminum derivatives (an ingredient found in most commercial baking powders and believed toxic by some).

I use active dry yeast for breads, because the fresh yeasts usually contain a preservative. One brand I especially like is called SAF yeast, a French yeast, which can be stored tightly wrapped in the freezer for about a year and spooned out when needed. I like its flavor, and it rises very consistently. The best place to find it is a specialty foods store.

In the Oven

Cookies, cakes, and breads should almost always be baked in the upper third of a conventional oven, to prevent the bottom surface of the baked goods from browning too quickly. An exception would be an oven that has the heating element on the top; in that case, do your baking in the middle of the oven. Another exception is a convection oven, which distributes heat evenly throughout and is made for baking eliminating the need for special placement. Convection ovens cook faster than conventional ovens, however, so you'll need to reduce baking times according to manufacturer's directions.

Another exception to the upper third rule is pizza. If the heating element of your oven is located on the bottom, pizza bakes in just a few minutes and browns beautifully when baked on the bottom rack. If you have a pizza stone, you can place it directly on the floor of the oven (below the bottom rack as long as the heating element is underneath, not on top of, the oven floor), and slide the dough onto it with a large wooden paddle, called a peel.

Glossary of Foods and Uses

Agar-agar Made from a type of seaweed, agar-agar is used as a thickening and gelling agent. You can even make a vegetarian gelatin with it. It comes in powder or flakes, and occasionally pressed into a bar. Follow individual package directions to produce the desired gelling strength.

Arrowroot The powdered root of an American plant, mainly used for thickening. It is easy to digest (remember arrowroot biscuits for babies?), and can be used teaspoon for teaspoon to replace cornstarch or flour in sauces and gravies.

Bragg's Liquid Aminos A seasoning made from soy, which looks like soy sauce, but with a taste all its own. Especially good in soups or to season rice or other grains.

Carob Also called St. John's bread. The pods of a Mediterranean tree are ground into a sweet, chocolatey-looking powder. It's considered a chocolate substitute, though it doesn't taste that much like chocolate. however, it is very good, and is a great replacement for people who can't eat chocolate. It can be made into cakes, candies, and brownies. Try our carob shake (see page 21). Carob contains no caffeine and is high in calcium.

Cheese Alternative Several companies make soy cheese, but many of them contain some lactose, making them still problematic for those who can't or don't want to eat dairy products.

Follow Your Heart now offers Vegan Gourmet Cheese Alternative: dairy free, all natural, and it melts! I even fooled my kids with it; they thought it was the real thing. Available nationally, or we'll ship it (see Resources, page 195). It comes in Cheddar, Nacho, Jack, and Mozzarella varieties.

Chicory, endive, and related greens
The chicory family includes slightly bitter greens that are used in salads and sometimes cooked. This includes Belgian endive, which is not to be confused with that other endive (also in the chicory family) called curly endive, or the smaller leafed frisée. Both kinds of endive can be used in salads, but Belgian endive is cultivated chiefly for its wide, mostly white leaves, which are fairly large and great for dipping and filling. Curly endive is that fluffy, pleasantly bitter green with curly, spear-shaped leaves that are chiefly used in salad mixes. Its less curly cousin, escarole, is also used in salads or can be briefly sautéed. Another chicory family member, radicchio, adds deep purple color to salads, and can also be sautéed, as in Sautéed Spinach and Radicchio (page 78).

Fresh heads of Belgian endive should be firm and full, with nice pale green or yellow tips. If they're beginning to brown or are torn, don't use them. Belgian endive also comes in a reddish/purple variety, which is very pretty—in that case the tips should be dark purplish and smooth.

Egg replacer
An ingenious product designed to replace eggs in recipes. Ener-G Egg Replacer brand is a powder made of all natural ingredients. When mixed with water, it helps provide the thickening and rising properties of eggs in recipes. You can't make an omelet with it, but it's great for baking.

Flour and Grain Alternatives
These are just a sample; there are more, and I encourage you to experiment. Each grain's flavor is unique.

Cornmeal
Available in several forms. Polenta is ground dried corn used for making polenta or cornmeal mush. Stone-ground cornmeal, made from yellow corn, is more like a flour and is great for making cornbread. White cornmeal has had the bran and germ removed, and is also used for cornbread. Blue cornmeal is the ground whole flour from blue-colored corn.

Quinoa flour
A nice golden color, and a whole grain product; similar to rice flour in its baking properties. Quinoa, a tiny South American grain, has the most protein of any of the world's grains. It has a delicious nutty flavor.

Rice flour
Brown (whole grain) and white rice flours are both available in natural food stores; white rice flour can sometimes be found at supermarkets and Asian groceries. Rice flour is gluten free, and is great in pancakes, cakes, crumb crusts, and gravies.

Rye flour
contains gluten, and is heavier to work with than wheat, but adds a nice flavor in small quantities. Available in whole grain form or as white rye flour.

Spelt flour
An ancient and non-hybridized cousin of wheat, this flour is readily available at natural food stores in its whole grain form. White spelt flour is sometimes available or can be ordered from Vita-Spelt; ask your natural foods retailer. It's expensive, but bakes up a lot like

wheat. Spelt does contain gluten, though it contains less gluten than wheat. I find it makes excellent cakes and pastries, but the texture of it in bread and pizza isn't as exciting as wheat—it doesn't stretch or rise as well. In a recipe calling for wheat flour, it usually takes a little more spelt flour as a substitute—about 2 tablespoons more per cup of flour.

Sylvan Farms general purpose flour Available at natural food stores, this is a combination of several alternative flours that are wheat free and imitate all-purpose flour in recipes. I've used it with good results in pie crusts, pancakes, cookies, and scones.

Kudzu or kuzu Similar to arrowroot, this white root is a thickener, and in traditional Japanese medicine is used to aid digestion. It usually comes in small lumps that need to be crushed before measuring.

Miso A traditional Japanese food made of fermented soybeans and salt, often with rice or barley added. It comes as a thick paste, and adds a salty, somewhat sweet, almost meaty flavor to soups and sauces. Because it is fermented and aged, it is very easy to digest, and if your miso is unpasteurized, the live culture imparts beneficial bacteria to the digestive tract, similar to yogurt. Simple Miso Soup (page 103) is a great vegetarian replacement for chicken soup, especially if someone's not feeling well. The unpasteurized miso, which generally tastes sweeter, is in the refrigerator sections of natural food and Asian groceries. Pasteurized miso is in soft packages on the shelf, next to other Asian ingredients. It has a stronger, saltier taste. I like them both, and if I'm making miso soup, I often mix two or more kinds: pasteurized brown rice miso, which is dark brown, and unpasteurized white rice miso, which has a pale color. Heat miso gently (do not boil) to help keep the miso culture alive.

Hatcho miso is made from all soybeans and is quite strong. Mugi miso has barley added to the soybeans, and is a dark reddish brown, and less strong than hatcho. Genmai miso, the brown rice type, is milder tasting and is a great all-purpose miso—I always keep it on hand. Akamiso is off-white or light yellow in color and is quite sweet. It adds wonderful flavor to dressings and spreads, and a little is good added to soups.

Mori-Nu Pudding Mix The same company that manufactures tofu in boxes makes a pudding mix meant to be blended with their tofu. We use it as the pastry cream in our Mandala Fruit Tart (page 164). It comes in lemon, vanilla, and chocolate flavors and is available at natural food stores.

Oils and fats In general, the more natural and unrefined, the better. When oil is extracted from seeds, sometimes excess heat is applied, which damages the oil. Extra-virgin olive oil is best because it's made from the first pressing of the olives (yes, cheaper olive oils come from the second or third pressing of the same olives!) and is unheated. I use a lot of olive oil; I keep a bottle right next to my stove with a pouring spout, and use it for most sautéing.

When you heat oils, you don't want them to smoke; that means the pan's too hot. Again, heat damages the oil, and it doesn't taste very good after it's burned, either. Truly the best way to consume oils is unheated, as in salad dressings; but since we enjoy sautéed foods as well, we're careful not to overly heat the oils. Deep-fried foods are something we eat only occasionally.

Buy oils that are minimally processed. Look for notes on the label like, "not heat extracted," "unrefined," "mechanically pressed" or "expeller-pressed," "contains no trans-fatty acids," and "made without chemicals or solvents." Unfortunately the term "cold-pressed" isn't a guarantee of low heat processing.

Generally the darker the oil, the more natural it is, because it hasn't been as refined (unless it's toasted, like some sesame and walnut oils—toasting darkens them). When oils are processed, they may be heated, filtered, bleached, and even deodorized. We've gotten so used to the taste of bland oils that unrefined oils taste strong to us. Yet those stronger flavors can be incorporated into our cooking. I've learned to love the flavor of tasty, unrefined olive oils.

Oils should be stored at cool temperatures in a dark cupboard or even in the refrigerator if you need to store it for several months; I would only do this with a delicate oil that goes rancid quickly, like walnut. Oils are fragile and will become rancid with time and when exposed to heat. You'll know by the smell when this has occurred, in which case it is time to discard the oil. The less refined the oil, the more apt it is to spoil, although olive oil, when kept in a dark container in a cool place, keeps for months, even a couple of years, if it was purchased when freshly pressed. Olive oil is mostly monounsaturated, which means it breaks down less quickly than a polyunsaturated oil.

I don't buy hydrogenated margarine, also known as a trans fat, which has had hydrogen bubbled through it to make it hard, like butter. The resulting synthetic polymers that are created are like nothing in nature, and recently, consumption of trans fats has been indicated in causing heart disease.

Butter is far better, to my mind, than hydrogenated margarine, because it's a natural product. Buy unsalted organic butter, natural, unrefined oils, and non-hydrogenated margarine. If you'd like to know more about this, read the definitive book on the subject, *Fats that Heal, Fats that Kill* by Udo Erasmus.

Rice: Arborio and **Basmati** Arborio rice is a short-grain, starchy white rice from Italy that is especially suited for making creamy risottos. India is the original home of Basmati rice, a fragrant long-grain rice available in brown or white forms.

Rice wrappers are somewhat see-through sheets of rice starch that have been rolled, pressed, and dried. When moistened, they become pliable and are used to wrap foods such as Spring Rolls (page 12). They are available at Asian groceries and some supermarkets.

Soymilk and **other alternative milks** Soymilk is a liquid made from cooked, filtered soybeans, with water and sometimes sweetener and flavorings added. The protein and carbohydrate contents are similar to cow's milk, depending on the manufacturer and what flavorings have been added. Fat contents vary. You can use it to replace cow's milk in many recipes. I often prefer its slightly nutty flavor. It is not generally as creamy tasting as whole milk, however. You can buy soymilk fresh in the dairy section, or on the shelf in aseptic boxes. Fresh soymilk is not as creamy, but I prefer it for baking. It tastes, well, fresher, and has a stronger "bean" flavor. The aseptically packaged milks are better in your coffee, and for drinking. Really, it's all a matter of taste.

Also available are **Almond milk, Rice milk,** and **Multigrain beverages.** Most of these are lower in protein than cow's milk or soymilk, so check the label. Again, you'll have to try some of each to see which ones you like. There are many new products of this line coming on the market.

Seitan (Wheatmeat) Seitan is the Japanese name for the "meat" of wheat—it's the protein portion of wheat. I made this once by hand, and it's a lot of work, and now I don't mind buying it instead. You make a dough from whole wheat flour, then knead and rinse it and knead and rinse it ad infinitum until all the starch is washed away, and the protein is what's left. Then it's seasoned and cut into cubes. I haven't done this in about 20 years, so don't follow my directions if you want to try it yourself go find a good macrobiotic cookbook.

Or go to your natural food store. Packaged in the deli case near the tofu, you'll find seasoned or plain seitan, or various wheatmeat products. They may be flavored with ginger, soy sauce, or even vegetarian "chicken" or "beef" flavors. I have also seen these products frozen. They're high in protein, and have a chewy texture and hearty flavor that is indeed meaty. Seitan has been used for a long time in Japan, where it is used in vegetarian Buddhist temple cooking.

Sweeteners Most of these items will need to be purchased at a natural foods store:

Brown rice syrup A mild sweetener made from cooking and refining brown rice. It can be used similarly to honey but is not as sweet.

Date sugar A coarse, dark brown sugar made from simply grinding dried dates.

Fruit source A combination of grape juice concentrate and rice syrup, it is less sweet than sugar and absorbed more slowly into the bloodstream. Available in liquid and granular forms.

Fruit syrup You can sometimes purchase fruit sweeteners made from a blend of fruit concentrates, such as peach and pineapple. They are refrigerated; one brand is Mystic Lake Dairy. Use as a substitute for honey or rice syrup.

Honey The liquid product of bees. I like to use mild honeys like clover and orange blossom for most baking, but you may enjoy the more assertive flavor of wildflower honey. Every region of the world has its own particular honeys and the flavors vary accordingly.

Maple sugar A dried form of maple syrup. Delicious, and can be exchanged cup for cup with regular sugar, but expensive.

Maple syrup The more common form of maple sweetener. I like to purchase grade "B" syrup, which is darker and thicker and has a stronger maple flavor.

Sucanat A less refined form of cane sugar, organically grown and unbleached. Tastes like a slightly stronger brown sugar.

Unbleached organic cane sugar Use cup for cup instead of regular sugar in recipes. It's a beige color because it isn't bleached, but it comes in small crystals like conventional sugar, and tastes much the same.

Tempeh A traditional Indonesian food and another good vegetarian protein source, though it is not as high in protein as tofu. Soybeans are fermented with friendly bacteria, which grows and holds the beans together into a chewy, nutty-tasting patty. While this food is strange to many of us, remember that we already eat many aged and/or fermented foods, such as cheese, yogurt, and wine. Actually, tempeh can be delicious, and we've included our recipes for Tempeh Tacos (page 94) and Bye-Bye Birdie (page 86) to prove it. The flavor of the different brands varies considerably. My favorite tempeh is made by Surata Soyfoods Co-op, but other tasty brands may be available in your area. Sometimes tempeh is mixed with grains as well as soybeans. Like tofu, it takes marinades and flavorings quite well.

Tofu is made from soymilk, which has been curdled and pressed into a white rectangle, somewhat like cheese. It can be quite firm or delicately soft, or anything in between, depending on the style of tofu and the manufacturer, and on how much water has been pressed out of the tofu. Unlike cheese, it doesn't melt, neither is it aged or fermented. It is very high in protein, in fact one of the best vegetarian protein sources, and is versatile in cooking. It usually comes packed in water in plastic tubs when it's fresh, or in aseptic boxes that don't need refrigeration. Soybeans contain natural oil, and some tofus have their fat reduced. Let's look at the different types of tofu and their uses:

Extra-firm tofu Use in Marinated Tofu (page 139) or in stir-fries, where it will definitely hold its shape. Some people prefer its chewier, denser texture. Because it has had more water pressed out of it, it absorbs marinades more readily.

Firm tofu is the best one to cut into squares for miso soup. It's the most commonly used. It makes a great Scrambled Tofu (page 48) or Chinese Tofu Salad (page 54). Also good in lasagne as a ricotta cheese replacement, when a firmer texture than silken is desired. It's often blended and used in tofu cheesecakes.

Mori-Nu tofu is packaged in aseptic boxes, so it needs no refrigeration until you open it. It comes in firm and extra-firm textures, but keep in mind that because of the way it's made, it is much softer than fresh tofu. It is very smooth and mild tasting, and comes in regular and "lite" (low fat). I love using this one in puddings and custards, though you can use the extra-firm in miso soup and many other applications. Try it in the pastry cream for our Mandala Fruit Tart (page 164).

Seasoned tofu Usually golden brown in color, this is tofu that has been marinated in seasonings and baked to make it very firm. It's an easy addition to salads and sandwiches because it's ready to eat. It comes in a variety of flavors such as savory, teriyaki, or spicy. We use it in our Spring Rolls (page 12), Chinese Tofu Salad (page 54), and Easier Caesar (page 60).

Soft or silken tofu is very tender, almost gelatinous; it is useful in puddings, or blended to make creamy sauces and salad dressings. It can also be crumbled into lasagne in place of ricotta cheese.

Vegenaise Follow Your Heart's own Vegenaise took years to develop. It's not easy making an egg-less mayo, but the results are incredible—it tastes really good, and is thick and creamy to boot. Follow Your Heart Vegenaise is available in the refrigerator section of most natural food stores and some supermarkets. It's made with your choice of canola, grapeseed, or soy oil. If you can't find it locally, call us, and we'll assist you in finding it. You can also check our Web site for a product locator. Reach us at www.followyourheart.com; look under "where to buy," or by phone at 818-348-0291.

Wheat flour There are several different types of wheat flours, and it pays to know their purposes and characteristics. It will make a big difference in your baking results.

All-purpose flour is the most commonly found flour in homes and recipes. It's a middle-of-the-road flour, with a gluten content of around 11 percent, and is usually made from hard winter wheat. It is white flour. Buy it unbleached—it's less processed. It's usually the best flour for making cakes and cookies, but it is fine for many breads and pie pastry as well. That's why they call it all-purpose! It is a mystery to me why no natural foods company, at this writing, makes an all-purpose flour that is organically grown or made from whole wheat. **Pastry flours**, made from soft winter wheat, have the lowest gluten content of all, around 9 percent. In pastry, cake, and cookie making, you want enough gluten to hold your dough together, but not enough to make it tough. Gluten is also the reason why you don't want to overhandle tender pastries—the more handling, the more it develops, which is great for bread but bad news for pie. **Whole wheat pastry flour** is made of soft white winter wheat, still containing its bran and germ. It is the whole grain flour of choice for cookies, cakes, pies, and pastries. **White pastry flour** is hard to find but can be special ordered (see Resources, page 195). It makes delicate pastries such as pie dough, but is a little too soft for most cakes and cookies on its own. **Cake flour** is made from soft white winter wheat that has had the bran and germ removed, and has also been bleached and bromated, which makes a better texture and structure for cakes. It's a very refined product so I don't use it often, or in this book; it does make very light and tender cakes, though.

Bread flour, made from hard red spring wheat, is the flour of choice for making breads and pizza. It has the highest gluten (protein) content of all the flours, 12 to 14 percent. The gluten in the wheat is what makes a nice stretchy dough and a chewy structure. **Whole wheat bread flour** still contains the bran and the germ of the wheat kernel. In **white bread flour** the bran and germ have been removed. Often in natural food stores you'll see this flour in 5-pound sacks or bulk bins marked, "Unbleached white flour" or simply "White flour." If it doesn't say pastry or all-purpose flour in the title, assume that it is bread flour. Sometimes on the package you'll see in fine print, "Best for bread."

If you love to bake, you may want to experiment with mixing different types of flour to achieve desired results. Note also that the percentages of protein will vary in flour, especially in different parts of the country. Often the protein content is indicated on the package.

Wheatmeat See Seitan.

Zest When a recipe calls for orange peel or lemon peel it is referring to the whole peel of an orange or lemon, including the pithy white part; zest means the colored part only, which has the flavor without the bitterness. A special tool called a zester helps to remove the zest only, cutting it into fine strips, or you can grate the citrus carefully, avoiding the white part of the peel. You can also carefully peel the zest using a regular peeler or paring knife; usually it is then cut into fine pieces.

Resources and Suggested Reading

Resources

Follow Your Heart, 21825 Sherman Way, Canoga Park, CA 91303 Call 818-884-0291, or visit our Web site: www.followyourheart.com. We can ship our Vegenaise, Vegan Gourmet Cheese Alternative, and other products, or tell you where it's available in your area.

King Arthur Flour Many kinds of alternative flours can be ordered from King Arthur's "The Baker's Catalogue." This company specializes in baking. Call 800-827-6836 for a copy of their catalog, or online at www.bakerscatalogue.com. They make my favorite all-purpose flour.

Mystic Lake Dairy If you can't find the concentrated fruit sweetener made by this Washington company, they'll ship it to you. Call them at 425-868-2029, or online at www.mysticlakedairy.com.

Books

The Artful Vegan: Fresh Flavors from the Millennium Restaurant, by Eric Tucker, Bruce Enloe, and Amy Pearce. Elevates vegan cooking to the art that it is. Inspiring photographs.

Chez Panisse Pizza, Pasta, and Calzone, by Alice Waters, Patricia Curtan, and Martine Labro. Fabulous pizza crust, unusual and creative toppings. I also recommend *Chez Panisse Vegetables,* and *Chez Panisse Fruits.*

Everyday Greens: Home Cooking from Greens, the Celebrated Vegetarian Restaurant, by Annie Sommerville. Innovative, international cooking from Greens Restaurant in San Francisco.

Cookbooks by Deborah Madison. Most recently she has published *Local Flavors: Cooking and Eating from America's Farmer's Markets* and *Vegetarian Cooking for Everyone.* I've enjoyed all her books, including *This Can't Be Tofu, The Greens Cookbook,* and *The Savory Way.* Madison makes great use of herbs and spices and produce in season.

Follow Your Heart's Vegetarian Soup Cookbook, by Janice Cook Migliaccio, Follow Your Heart Press, 2002. Fifty of our favorite soup recipes.

The Joy of Cooking, by Rombauer and Becker, and *The All New Joy of Cooking,* by Rombauer, Becker, and Becker. Among these two books can be found just about every basic recipe you ever wanted; the *The All New Joy of Cooking* includes many ethnic, Asian, and contemporary recipes that we currently enjoy. If I had to be stranded on a desert island with only one cookbook, it would be one of these, probably the older one.

Martha Stewart Living Magazine. I find more great recipes in this magazine, many of them vegetarian, even containing tofu. The recipes often reflect current health information, as well.

The Moosewood Cookbooks. I have the original *Moosewood Cookbook* by Mollie Katzen, but many more have been published. They've made a great contribution to vegetarian cuisine over the years.

The Vegetarian Epicure, Books I & II, and *The New Vegetarian Epicure,* by Anna Thomas. Vegetarian classics, fun to read, and the recipes work.

The Vegetarian Grill: 200 Recipes for Inspired Flame-Kissed Meals, by Andrea Chesman. Creative and delicious ways to cook every kind of vegetable. Grilled pizza, too.

A Year in a Vegetarian Kitchen: Easy Seasonal Dishes for Family and Friends, by Jack Bishop. The *Cook's Magazine* writer offers creative seasonal fare. Fun to read.

Index